Best Friends

Living Today in Alateen

Al-Anon Family Groups

hope for families and friends of alcoholics

AL-ANON BOOKS AND ISBN LISTINGS:

Alateen—Hope for Children of Alcoholics
0-910034-20-6

The Dilemma of the Alcoholic Marriage
0-910034-18-4

The Al-Anon Family Groups—Classic Edition
0-910034-36-2

One Day at a Time in Al-Anon
0-910034-21-4
0-910034-63-X Large Print

Lois Remembers
0-910034-23-0

Al-Anon's Twelve Steps & Twelve Traditions
0-910034-24-9

Alateen—a Day at a Time
0-910034-53-2

As We Understood...
0-910034-56-7

...In All Our Affairs: Making Crises Work for You
0-910034-73-7

Courage to Change—One Day at a Time in Al-Anon II
0-910034-79-6
0-910034-84-2 Large Print

How Al-Anon Works for Families & Friends of Alcoholics
0-910034-28-3

Courage to Be Me
0-910034-30-3

Paths to Recovery—Al-Anon's Steps, Traditions and Concepts
0-910034-31-1

Living

TODAY

in Alateen

Al-Anon Family Groups
hope for families and friends of alcoholics

For information and catalog of literature write:

Al-Anon Family Group Headquarters, Inc.
1600 Corporate Landing Parkway
Virginia Beach, VA 23454-5617
Phone: (757) 563-1600 Fax: (757) 563-1655
http://www.al-anon.alateen.org
E-mail: wso@al-anon.org

© Al-Anon Family Group Headquarters, Inc. 2001

Al-Anon/Alateen is supported by members' voluntary contributions
and from the sale of our Conference Approved Literature.

Library of Congress Control No. 2001130371
ISBN-0-910034-38-9

Publisher's Cataloging In Publication
Al-Anon Family Group Headquarters, Inc.
Living today in Alateen / Al-Anon Family Groups, Inc.
    Includes index.
    ISBN 0-910034-38-9
    LCCN 2001130371
    1. Alcoholics—Family relationships. 2. Children of Alcoholics
3. Al-Anon Family Group Headquarters, Inc.

Approved by
World Service Conference
Al-Anon Family Groups

1-50M-01-10.00   B-26   Printed in U.S.A.

Alateen, part of the Al-Anon Family Groups, is a fellowship of young people whose lives have been affected by alcoholism in a family member or close friend. We help each other by sharing our experience, strength, and hope.

We believe alcoholism is a family disease because it affects all the members emotionally and sometimes physically. Although we cannot change or control our parents, we can detach from their problems while continuing to love them.

We do not discuss religion or become involved with any outside organizations. Our sole topic is the solution of our problems. We are always careful to protect each other's anonymity as well as that of all Al-Anon and AA members.

By applying the Twelve Steps to ourselves, we begin to grow mentally, emotionally, and spiritually. We will always be grateful to Alateen for giving us a wonderful, healthy program to live by and enjoy.

The Suggested Alateen Preamble to the Twelve Steps

Introduction

Living Today in Alateen is a collection of personal sharings from Alateen members around the world. Alateens are young people whose lives have been affected by someone else's drinking. The following pages show ways that Alateen members reach out to people their own age. They share experience, strength, and hope without judging themselves or anyone else.

In this book, Alateens share how they live right now, today. They can remember what happened yesterday and think about it if they want to, but they know it isn't necessary to live in the past. The future does not exist yet, so it isn't necessary for them to spend a lot of time thinking about the future, either.

By living today in Alateen, young people decide how to find contentment and even happiness, whether the alcoholic is still drinking or not.

There are separate pages for each day of the year. There is also a subject index to help find pages about certain feelings, ideas, and Alateen tools. The tools of the Alateen program are to help us feel better about who we are right now, today.

The New Year is here. It feels like a new beginning. It's as if my slate has been cleaned and I can start all over.

Like most people I know, I find myself making at least one New Year's resolution. Due to my family history with alcoholism, my resolutions in the past have been more about changing someone else. I constantly focused on improving them. I really thought that I could change other people and tried my best to do so. Putting all my attention on others allowed me to overlook my own flaws.

The program teaches me to concentrate on improving myself. I use the slogan "Live and Let Live" during this time of year. It is a kind of reality check for me and it makes me aware of my biggest flaw—control.

Things to Think About

Where do I want to put my focus during the coming year?

My parents have been divorced for six years. I recently learned that my father has had a chronic drinking problem for at least 20 years. He has been in rehabilitation many times, but has always relapsed. My dad knows that I hate his drinking.

Through the program, I have learned to accept my father's drinking as his problem, not mine. I had nothing to do with it. As much as I hate it, I have to accept his alcoholism as reality. Today I can choose not to be around him when he is drinking.

Acceptance is working Step One. It is admitting that I am powerless over someone or something. I try to accept everything that comes, even though it may not be what I want. At the same time, I have to remember that I have choices about removing myself from unacceptable behavior.

Things to Think About

Acceptance allows me to live in reality and makes healthy decisions possible.

I come from a long line of alcoholics. I remember a lot of things that my alcoholic father did that I wish I didn't have to remember. When I was young, my father was not drinking, but his alcoholism ruled my world. He seemed unable to make rational decisions. When I was seven years old, his job moved us across the country. This left me with no one safe to share my feelings with about my family, so I stuffed everything.

Now all of the resentments and anger toward my father are coming out, and he doesn't understand why. With the help of my Alateen group, the Steps, and the Traditions, I am learning to deal with my feelings instead of stuffing them. I now know that instead of trying to reason with my father, I can detach. I understand that it's not my fault he is an alcoholic and that I deserve to be happy regardless of his actions.

Things to Think About

"Resentments mark the places where I see myself as a victim."

Courage to Change, p. 352

Before I got to Alateen, there was a lot of fighting in my home. I felt torn between my parents. My father was the alcoholic in my life, but my mother did not attend Al-Anon. When they fought, I felt as if it were my responsibility to make them stop. But when I got into the middle of it, I only seemed to make things worse.

When I came to Alateen, I learned to back off, mind my own business, and let them talk it out themselves. I am not responsible for stepping in and trying to fix other people's problems. I need to learn how to solve my own problems.

Things to Think About

"Live and Let Live" has helped me to live my own life, work my own program, and stay out of my parents' business.

A puzzle page in a newspaper showed a colorful sketch of an underwater scene with the question, "Can you find the starfish in the sketch?" At first sight, the scene looked like a drawing of a clump of seaweed. When I looked again, I spotted a fish chewing at some coral, a fat sea cucumber crawling across the sand, and a shrimp nearby. But where was the starfish? A closer examination revealed the starfish concealed in seaweed. It was hidden, but it was there. After I discovered the starfish, the drawing was never the same. The drawing had not changed, but my new perception gave the sketch more meaning.

In the same way, I searched for something or someone in my life to give me courage, strength, and hope to continue living. Finally I found Alateen, and my life has never been the same. As with the sketch, nothing changed but my perception. Alateen gave my life meaning, and I began to look at the positive.

Today I'm a happier person. I move through life with a smile—a smile that replaced the tears. Thank you, Alateen.

Things to Think About

How has Alateen changed the way I look at life?

I used to get angry at my friends very easily. If someone said something I didn't like, I would give him or her dirty looks for the rest of the day. I wouldn't tell anyone why I was angry, and no one would know for sure who I was angry with.

After I started Alateen, I learned a lot about how I react to others. Now I work on having more patience. I know that I can't control what others do, but I can control my reaction to what they do. To really communicate, I need to talk directly to other people. When I'm angry I can tell my friends why I'm angry, and we can talk it out.

Things to Think About

"I've grown enough in Al-Anon to realize that the look, tone, or mood of another person toward me often has nothing to do with me. It generally has more to do with what is going on inside the other person."

Courage to Change, p. 320

Step One says we admitted we were power-less over alcohol. Today I work this Step by changing "alcohol" to "people and places." I used to think I had control over everybody—the alcoholic and everyone else. I thought that I could make them change into who I wanted them to be. Now I understand that I am powerless over other people. The only person I can change is me.

Alateen helped me understand the concept of powerlessness. Today when I notice I'm slipping back into trying to control, I stop and remember Step One.

Things to Think About

"When I worry about things I can't control, I'm only hurting myself. Alateen helps me to stop worrying about other people and their lives so I can make the most of mine."

Alateen—a Day at a Time, p. 111

For me letting go of other people's problems is

the hardest thing to learn. I have a lot of friends who are being affected by alcoholism, and I let their problems affect me.

The reason I say that letting go is so hard for me to do is because early in the program, I thought I was using a slogan. I would say, "Live and Let Live" and try to forget about the problem.

At my first Alateen round-up, I broke through my denial. Instead of truly letting go, I had been stuffing everything. My worries were still there and were made worse by the pressure of keeping them inside. I have to continue to work Steps One, Two, and Three until I can truly accept that my friends are all God's children and can be helped if they are willing to reach out.

Things to Think About

My challenge is to work on myself and let God take care of my friends.

When my dad was drinking, he would come home late at night, get angry, and spank me and my brother for no reason at all. I thought my mom was crazy. She would be so upset about things that sometimes she would hit my brother, too.

Now my dad goes to AA and my mom goes to Al-Anon. My brother and I go to Alateen. We all go to lots of meetings. I'm grateful that today my mom doesn't act crazy and my dad isn't drinking. We all have sponsors to help us, but we each have to work our own program.

Whenever I get angry or sad, I call my sponsor. She listens to me and helps me to use Alateen tools like "Easy Does It" and "How Important Is It?" I can't just depend on my parents to make my life better. I have to do my part.

Things to Think About

Do I use a sponsor to help me work the program?

I met an Alateen member who answered my questions about what was going on in my house. Then he brought me to Alateen. Since that day, I have felt better and better. I received so much from the program and its members.

One day it was time for me to say good-bye to Alateen, because I wasn't a teenager anymore. At first I was angry and scared, but I overcame my fear and went to an Al-Anon meeting. Even though the members were older than I, it was the same program, and I could give my point of view as a child of an alcoholic. Members told me how much I helped them to understand their own children.

Now I'm an Alateen sponsor. I am giving something back to Alateen, but I still receive something in return. It's just another step in my recovery. There are so many ways I can still help Alateen. Sponsoring is just one of them. Looking at the newcomers reminds me what I was like before and how much I need the program. No matter whether it's Alateen or Al-Anon, we all use the same Twelve Steps.

Things to Think About

Do I think of Alateen as part of Al-Anon?

A situation facing me today is how to act around my sister when she gets back from reha-bilitation. I'm glad that she is alive today and that she will be home soon, but it scares me because I'm not sure how she is going to act. I'm afraid she will get back into some of the problems and situations that she was in before.

I have to concentrate on my program so that I can live without walking around on eggshells. I don't want to worry about saying or doing something that will offend her. Alateen teaches me that she is responsible for making her own decisions and I am responsible for making mine. I need to remember to let go and let God.

Things to Think About

"My life doesn't depend on whether the alcoholic is drinking or sober. I'm here to work on me. The program has the answers to my problems and gives me courage to work them out for myself."

Alateen—a Day at a Time, p. 106

When I went to my first meeting in Alateen, I didn't think I'd find anyone who had the same problems I did. I thought people would make fun of me because I was different. Instead all of them talked about their own problems, which sounded surprisingly like mine. They showed unconditional love for one another, and that was a strange experience for me.

Before Alateen   After Alateen

I've been in the program now for over a year. My fear of going to meetings has disappeared and I accept everyone in a special way. I think of them as my family. I can talk to them about anything, and they accept me for who I am. I owe a lot to Alateen. It has changed my life for the better.

Things to Think About

We are really much more alike than
we are different.

"First Things First" is a slogan that works well for me. The next time life throws problems at me too fast, I will try to remember  what Alateen has taught me. I don't have to take on all my problems at once. I can sort out what is really important and then deal with them one at a time.

First I must decide if a problem is really mine to solve. It may be someone else's problem, and I may need to let go. If it is my problem, then I can look for solutions. I can check to see what is my part. Do I need to change my attitude toward something, or is there something I need to accept? It's much easier to work things out when I'm willing to do my part.

Things to Think About

How has the slogan "First Things First" helped me?

I started going to Alateen because my sister asked me to come. My first feeling in the group was fear. I felt as though I was going to be judged.

 As I kept coming back and started listening to the Steps and paying attention to what people were really saying, my fear began to go away.

A few months later, I really started to get involved in my program. I picked a sponsor and began working the Steps with her. Working with my sponsor made my life easier. Problems that seemed so big came into perspective. It seemed easier to manage all my relationships, from my parents and siblings to school and friends. Alateen works!

When I take time to look at the whole picture, big things get smaller. I just need to take my time and look at things in their real perspective.

Things to Think About

Recovery is being willing to use the principles of Alateen in my daily living.

My brother is an alcoholic. He doesn't drink right now and he goes to a program. I used to feel guilty because I thought it was my responsibility to stop his drinking. I've gotten over my guilt. It's been hard, but after I acknowledged that it wasn't my fault he drank, it's been easier to detach from his problems.

Detachment really works for me. When I think something he is doing is my fault, I have to step out of myself for a moment. I ask myself if I can control the outcome of what is going to happen. Is it really my responsibility to tell my brother what to do? I've learned that I need to detach, concentrate on myself, and trust in my Higher Power to take care of him.

Things to Think About

"By practicing detachment, I can learn to accept and love myself again and pass that acceptance and love on to others."

Alateen—a Day at a Time, p. 194

Alateens share on their Higher Power:

• I used to think that God was a genie. He granted wishes, made some people happy, and ignored others. Now I know that isn't true. He's always there to hear my prayers and His responses are yes, no, or wait. By learning to trust and practicing patience, I know that He will do the best for me today.

• "Let Go and Let God" was one of the first slogans I heard when I joined Alateen. I would go around saying "Let Go and Let God," but I never really knew what it meant. After realizing this, I sat down and thought about that slogan. I decided it means giving things to God instead of getting upset about them. Today I will use this slogan instead of getting into a yelling match with my alcoholic father.

• When I think about my Higher Power, I feel free. I feel free from the pressures of everyday life, from the pain of the past, and from the fear of tomorrow. My Higher Power gives me the strength and courage to face the world. All I have to do is ask.

Things to Think About

What does my Higher Power mean to me?

Alateen literature helps me cool down when I'm mad. It helps me relax and it cheers me up. I feel pressure when I don't read my literature. My days don't go as well, and my life is not as happy. I feel the same way if I don't go to a meeting.

I feel like the Alateen books were planned with my life in mind. When I read a daily page, it sort of describes the problems I'm having that day, and I think that is totally cool. If I don't read that page, I miss out on directions from Alateen and I don't know where I'm going.

I am so grateful for our literature. It really helps me with my problems. My group reminds me why it's important to read it. Together, the group and the literature provide me with a path to follow.

Things to Think About

"Alateen is the key that unlocks the door of my confused mind. I have a program that helps me to make sense of my mixed-up thinking and feeling."

Alateen—a Day at a Time, p. 14

To me Alateen isn't just a group where I can go and talk about the problems of living with alcoholics. It's more like the family I've always wanted. I've never felt so much love before. At first this kind of closeness seemed kind of weird to me. I wasn't used to showing my emotions.

When I went to my first Alateen conference, it really blew my mind! Everyone loved everyone and no one was fighting—the experience changed me. It changed the way I look at life and the way I look at myself. I'm actually starting to love myself for who I am. For once I can say I'm proud of myself. I keep coming back and I always want to come back—I love it. I never have to be alone again.

I wish that Alateen was better known around the schools because a lot more kids could be getting help. Alateen straightened my life out, and I need to do my part in carrying the message.

Things to Think About

"Our great obligation is to those still in need. Leading another person from despair to hope and love brings comfort to both the giver and receiver."

Al-Anon/Alateen Service Manual, p. 10

Living with an alcoholic for so many years has left my mind full of bad memories. I remember the nights my dad would stumble in drunk and wake the house up with his screaming, ranting, and raving. I also remember crying myself to sleep.

Today I know it is okay to have my memories, but I choose not to let them hurt me. I can use my memories as a resource to help me deal with the present. When something from my past comes up, I can look back to understand. I can use my memories to share with others so that they can understand where I'm coming from. I can recognize my growth by remembering what I used to be like and how I've changed. I can be grateful. I can let go of the hurt and still keep the memories.

Things to Think About

"When I feel unable to move, or when I am filled with fear, I have a wonderful gift to help clear my way— the gift of memory. Too often my memory has given me sadness, bringing back past hurt and shame. But now I can use my memory to see the progress I have made and to know the joy of gratitude."

Courage to Change, p. 262

When I started in Alateen, I discovered that groups could have problems, too. My first Alateen group had a real problem being quiet and listening to each other. As I continued to attend meetings, I felt I was not being respected, so I wanted to quit. I talked to one of our sponsors about my feelings and asked what could be done. She told me I could ask for a group conscience meeting, but I was afraid to bring it up.

After a while, the problem happened again while I was chairing a meeting. This time I asked for a group conscience meeting and shared my feelings. It helped a great deal. After we talked about it, we made a decision about what is acceptable behavior in our group. Now others join in and support me if someone distracts the group. I've learned that I need to voice my opinion without letting other people run me off. I go to Alateen to receive help and I don't have to give up my meetings because of someone else's bad behavior.

Things to Think About

"Our common welfare should come first; personal progress for the greatest number depends upon unity."

Tradition One

The Third Step says to turn our will and our life over to the care of God as we understood Him. I had real trouble doing this because I didn't have a God!

I asked my sponsor about it, and he told me to make up something that I would understand and go with that, so I did. I didn't call him God or anything — I called him Joe. When I did the Third Step and turned my life and my will over to Joe, my life started to get better. Because I had a Higher Power of my own, I could tell him things that I knew he would understand—he was my personal God. Later in recovery, I started to call him God, but it was important to me in the beginning to know that I had the right to choose.

Things to Think About

"Many of us call this Higher Power 'God.' Some of us feel this is the group. It doesn't matter, as long as we really believe in something outside of ourselves that can help us."

Alateen—Hope for Children of Alcoholics, p. 14

Before I came to Alateen, I was very emotional and I didn't know how to deal with my problems.

 My dad would be drunk and act crazy. He would cuss at me, put me down, and physically abuse me. I would get so upset that I'd cry myself to sleep. I felt like a nothing.

Alateen has helped me build my self-esteem. I am not a nothing and I don't deserve to be treated badly. I found out that I'm not the only one who has to deal with this behavior and it's not my fault. My dad suffers from alcoholism, and I have been suffering as a result of his illness.

Today I can talk out my feelings, including anger. I've learned to accept my life as it is. I've learned to remove myself from dangerous situations and not participate in arguments. My choices may be limited, but I do have choices.

Things to Think About

"Problems are painful but I've got a way to handle them. When I share the hurt and get it outside of myself, the pain starts to go away and the healing begins."

Alateen—a Day at a Time, p. 302

I'm new to Alateen. Although I haven't begun to work the Steps, I can already see that Alateen has made a difference in my life. Prior to coming to Alateen meetings, I thought my home life was unbearable. My father drinks, and although I didn't think it affected me, I knew it gave my mother problems, and her behavior affected me. By the time I began coming to Alateen, the relationship between my mother and me had gotten to the point that we couldn't be in the same room together.

The program allows me to talk about my problems to someone who is not directly involved and will only listen. I can share my feelings in safety. I realize now how the disease has affected my mother and how I am reacting to her. We are closer than we have ever been, and thanks to the program, grow closer every day. Alateen has given me the patience and understanding I need to help repair my relationship with my mother.

Things to Think About

"Each Alateen Group has but one purpose: to help other teenagers of alcoholics. We do this by practicing the Twelve Steps of AA ourselves and by encouraging and understanding the members of our immediate families."

Alateen Tradition Five

Knowing how I behave, why I am the way I am, and understanding that the disease is the cause makes life more manageable. I realize that I'm not crazy and I don't have to be alone. For growth, I am patient, willing, and ready. I try to stick with the program throughout the good

One Day at a Time

times and the bad times and never give up on myself. I am patient because things don't change overnight. It works if I work it, but God and I do it together. I could never have imagined the happiness and peace that I get from the program, from letting go and letting God and working my program one day at a time.

Things to Think About

"Yesterday is history, tomorrow is mystery, today is God's gift to you. That's why it's called the present."

The Forum, April 1996, p. 13

Alateen helps me even when alcoholism is not involved. Today a couple of friends kept calling me and wouldn't stop. They were aggravating me all morning, and I was getting so worked up that I started to get sick. I tried using the slogan "Easy Does It" for a while, but it still bothered me. Finally I thought about "Think" and used a different  approach. I told them how I was feeling about what they were doing. They said they were sorry and stopped calling, but even if they hadn't, I had said what I needed to say for me.

I've learned from this that if the first slogan I use doesn't work, I shouldn't give up. I'll try another slogan and work toward my own serenity rather than trying to change other people's behavior.

Things to Think About

"Sometimes I talk first and think later and it gets me into trouble. Alateen helps me to turn that around. Using the slogan 'Think' helps me think before I act and keeps me from saying and doing things I'll be sorry for later."

Alateen—a Day at a Time, p. 113

Alateens share on coping with alcoholism:

• Today I'm in a happy place. Things still don't always go my way, but I'm much better at coping. Without this program, I don't know where I would be. Thank you, Alateen.

• In Alateen I learned that alcoholism is a family disease. My group helped me realize that the alcoholic wasn't the only sick person in my family. Now I can look at things with a different perspective. I just have to keep in mind that I can't control the people around me. Once I realize that, things run more smoothly.

• Acceptance is easier when it is what I want to do. I've been working with the thought "Get out of God's way – I may be slowing Him down."

Things to Think About

"The family often ends up being just as obsessed with the alcoholic's drinking as he is, only they are trying to figure out how to stop it, and he is trying to figure out how to keep it up."

Alateen—Hope for Children of Alcoholics, p. 6

Just for Today

I thought there was no hope for my brother. I tried everything, even Alateen, but it didn't seem to help. I decided that I had to talk to him face-to-face. I was so scared! I told him how much his behavior scared me. I told him I wanted him to stop drinking because I loved him and didn't want him to die. He said he would stop, but a week later he did it again. Then it hit me; the things I learned at Alateen started to fall in place. I can't make him stop. It is his choice.

He recently went into treatment again, and I've been working the Steps and using the tools of the program. I hope my brother will be different when I see him again, but what I need to do is concentrate on changing his sister—me. "Just for Today" helps me concentrate on today only, and not on what might happen.

Things to Think About

"Realizing 'whose problem is whose' is having the wisdom to know the difference between what I can change and what I have to accept. Other people's problems are mine only when I don't know, or don't want to know, the difference."

Alateen—a Day at a Time, p. 247

Alateens share on the slogans that help them work their program:

• My favorite slogan is "Together We Can Make It." Through Alateen I've learned that I can't always work things out on my own; sometimes I need the help of others. By sharing what I have to say and listening to what others have to say, I learn how to deal with some of my problems.

• "Let Go and Let God" is my favorite slogan. I use it when my mom starts rushing around. When she rushes, I know she will get mad, so I start feeling scared. Saying "Let Go and Let God" reminds me to turn my mom's behavior over to God.

• "Think" is my favorite slogan. I use it when I have to make a decision or say something important. When I think before I talk, I usually get things right. "Think!"

• When I first came to Alateen, I felt scared and nervous. I had so many problems on my mind that I was ready to cry. The slogan "Easy Does It" helped me a lot. It taught me to slow down and stay in today.

Things to Think About

What slogan have I used recently?

Many times I wonder where I would be without this program and I come to the conclusion that I probably wouldn't be alive.

Alateen is a large part of the life I've been given. Through the past year, I've come to see my Higher Power as someone who actually works in my life. Besides putting me in a program where I am loved and emotionally stable, my Higher Power has also given me people — people in the meeting rooms and conferences, people who live all over the world and have problems like mine. He has put sponsors in my life who help me improve my relationships and inter-actions with other people.

As I continue my life, I know that even through the most difficult times there are two people who will always be and have always been there for me—my Higher Power and me.

Things to Think About

"As I decide what is and isn't acceptable for me, I learn to live protected without walls."

Courage to Change, p. 201

As I grew up, I never knew how to accept anything. I would scream if I didn't get my way and 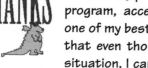 hold grudges against anyone who crossed my path. After being in the program, acceptance has become one of my best tools. I have learned that even though I may not like a situation, I can accept it and learn how to cope with it.

My stepfather was a member of AA and he instilled three ideas in my head: acceptance, laughter, and patience. He is now deceased, but in his memory I am determined to try to show my appreciation for what he taught me. I try to accept things in my life and to focus on what I can do to improve myself.

Acceptance can be a difficult concept to grasp. It doesn't mean liking, understanding, or even supporting a situation. But if I can accept a situation, I have the power to better my outlook and improve things for myself and possibly for others. Acceptance allows me to have power over myself instead of having the situation control me.

Things to Think About

What is something I need to accept?

My dad used to drink and then get angry. I'd get scared and hide from him. I hoped he would stop drinking, but he didn't. Later my mom and dad divorced, and then he remarried. During this time, I was mad and I thought I couldn't depend on anybody but me. I didn't know  how to let God help me, so I did things that got me into a lot of trouble.

Since I've been to Alateen meetings, I've gotten better and I'm not so scared. My life is much happier and I've learned to pray for help in making decisions. I have people to depend on when I need help. I can call my sponsor or other teens at my meeting and talk about things before I make a decision.

Things to Think About

"Only after we have done our best, without rationalizing, can we calm down and 'Let Go and Let God.'"

Alateen—Hope for Children of Alcoholics, p. 49

Before I came to Alateen, I always fought with my stepdad. Both of us knew exactly what to do in order to make the other one mad. I used to scream and yell at him until he sent me to my room and grounded me.

Today we still disagree, but I don't have to scream and yell. I can go to my room and call my sponsor or read my Alateen books. After I do that, I can calmly talk to him and we can resolve our problem.

By working with a sponsor and reading the literature, I can talk out my problems with my parents without blowing up in their faces. Learning to change the things I can, such as my behavior, makes my life more peaceful. For that I am truly grateful to Alateen.

Things to Think About

Things to Think About

"Courage was something I always wanted, and now I have some of it—thanks to working on myself and not others."

The Forum, March 1999, p. 12

The Alateen tool that helps me the most is the Serenity Prayer. I can say it whenever I feel confusion and frustration.

Gradually Alateen helps me realize that my problem is much deeper than I ever realized. Alateen helps me understand that I am powerless over what happened to me when I was younger and that the best thing I can do for myself is to forgive. The past is past,  and unless I let go of it, the past is where I live.

Looking back today, I realize that Alateen saved my life. It gave me the chance to truly live.

Things to Think About

"God, grant me the serenity to accept the things I cannot change, courage to change the things I can, and wisdom to know the difference."

Serenity Prayer

Today I'm a grateful Alateen. Before I began going to meetings, I was very shy and afraid of people. I wondered what they would think about me if I talked to them and told them what I felt. I tried to be just like everyone else and couldn't. I was depressed and lonely, always looking at life in a negative way.

Alateen changed my lifestyle and my way of thinking. Now I don't try to be like anyone else; I try to be me. I'm more optimistic and happy. I have a couple of good friends who understand me and accept me just as I am. It feels great to be a part of this wonderful fellowship of Alateen. Friendship is a rare and precious jewel that I only appreciate when I share it with someone.

Things to Think About

"In Alateen I found love, friends, understanding, and faith—all the things I had lost."

Alateen Talks Back on Serenity, p. 21

Alateens share on dealing with anger:

• I used to get in a lot of trouble for getting into fights. If I wasn't fighting at school, I would be fighting with my dad. Since I've started coming to Alateen I've learned to deal with my anger in different ways. Instead of fighting, I'll walk away and then write my anger down on a piece of paper or call a friend and talk about it.

• I've found that I get angry at people because I've judged them. I have to give things and people a chance. First I need to know them and understand their situation. I can love them for who they are, not for how I would like them to be.

Things to Think About

"Now I realize that other people treat me the same way I treat them. If I want things to be different, it's up to me to change my attitude."

Alateen—a Day at a Time, p. 258

I love Alateen weekends because I feel so good afterward. I don't know where I would be today if it wasn't for Alateen.

Before I came to Alateen, I didn't understand

 my mother's drinking. I tried my best to get her to stop and she wouldn't—no matter how many times I asked. Today, because of Alateen, I understand it

doesn't matter that I want the alcoholic to quit drinking. When she is ready, she will realize that she has a problem, and then it will be her decision to get help. I can show her the path to sobriety, but the walk is up to her.

Living my program is the best thing that I can do for both of us. I can find peace and content-ment within myself and be a living example of the power of the Twelve Steps.

Things to Think About

"I may find it easy to point to the alcoholic's irrational or self-destructive choices. It is harder to admit that my own behavior has not always been sane. Today I can let go of insisting upon my will. With this simple decision, I make a commitment to sanity."

Courage to Change, p. 316

When I first came to Alateen, I was sure that it was a waste of time. Nothing could change the people in my life or make my life better. As far as I was concerned, I was just a victim and it was hopeless to think that things could ever change.

Now as I look back and see all the gifts I have been given through this program, I am filled with gratitude. I have been blessed with faith, hope, and courage. I've been taught how to use these gifts to get through the rough times. I don't always have choices over the circumstances of my life, but I do have choices over my reaction to those circumstances. I try to remember that each day is a present—a gift from God.

Things to Think About

"When I believe that someone or something else is in control of my attitude, let me remember that I'm always free to choose my reactions. The program helps me gain the freedom to make wise choices that are good for me."

Alateen—a Day at a Time, p. 61

I remember one time when I thought nothing was going right and I completely lost my serenity. Then I looked in the *Courage to Be Me* book and saw something that reminded me to work my program. It was a picture of a staircase on page 88 and it said, "Please take the Steps, as the elevator to serenity is not working." I was so happy that I  found something I understood. A few days later, I started my Fourth Step. So far it's been hard, but I've learned a lot about myself.

If I think that everything is too hard, I remember it doesn't have to be that hard. It just has to be hard enough to cause me to "Think!" I'm grateful to all of you who give me such encouragement in Alateen.

Things to Think About

What are some of the Alateen tools that help me think?

When I arrived at Alateen, I was a scared teenager with many problems that I didn't know how to solve. I came to my first meeting thinking that I would not come back. But instead of hiding behind my wall like usual, I opened my heart and trusted the group with one of my problems. Afterward everyone applauded. They shared similar experiences and how the program had helped them. I left feeling so good that I continued going to meetings. Although the problem itself was not a big deal, sharing about it was the beginning of my recovery.

I have to open my mind to the possibility of asking for help from a Higher Power. I need help standing on my own. To receive help, all I have to do is be willing and ask. I must remember that in Alateen the objective is not perfection, but continued personal improvement.

Things to Think About

"A Higher Power works through other people so I don't have to go looking for Him like a needle in a haystack. I just have to keep coming to meetings and sharing with the people there."

Alateen—a Day at a Time, p. 37

My grandmother told me that I was going to Alateen. I tried to ignore her, but the following  Monday I went to my first meeting. I thought it was fun! The meeting was about anger, love, and trust. I had a lot to say, but was too shy to talk. Now I'm more comfortable at meetings. I can talk a little, but I still don't talk all that much.

Sometimes I still feel angry when my mom breaks a promise. When she tells me she will do something, I think to myself, "It may not happen, so don't get your hopes up." Mostly I try to take things as they come. Because of Alateen, I know that my mom loves me to the best of her ability, even though I know that she can't always be trusted.

Things to Think About

"Acceptance does not mean we have to like all of it; it only means we have to realize that reality is reality."

From Survival to Recovery, p. 288

I want to talk about escape because that's what I used to do when something was on my mind. Sometimes escaping is okay, but if all I do is escape, it makes matters worse. Some people escape through television, music, or sleeping. My escape was running away from home. I escaped so much it was killing my social life, my grades, my pets, the non-alcoholic, and me. Basically my motto was "When the going gets tough, the tough pack their things and leave." That didn't help me or anyone else.

Alateen has taught me that there is a better way. I have choices about removing myself from the room or the house, but I can also call someone, read my literature, write in my journal, and try to apply a slogan like "How Important Is It?" All of these tools help me deal with the reality of my life without running away.

Things to Think About

How am I trying to escape from reality?

To me "One Day at a Time" means learning to face my problems one day at a time. It means allowing myself to take the time I need to resolve the troubles in my family or within myself. It means living in today only and not projecting how things will turn out in the future.

Nobody can eliminate a disease, and alcoholism is a disease that has affected my entire family. Once affected by it, the best I can do is slowly recover my health. I cannot heal from the effects overnight, and if I expect instant health, I will become frustrated and sad. Using the slogan "One Day at a Time" helps me. The people in Alateen and Al-Anon help me learn how to use this slogan. If I take my time and listen in the meetings, I can help myself and others recover from the effects of this disease.

Things to Think About

"If I feel unable to do something today, I trust that there will be another opportunity if it is something I am meant to do. It doesn't have to be now or never, all or nothing."

Courage to Change, p. 30

Alateens share on ways to cope with the family disease of alcoholism:

• My mom is the non-drinker, but I have to use the slogans to keep from reacting to her behavior. I must remember that she is affected by alcoholism, too.

• My sister and I are so much alike that we have trouble getting along. It's hard to accept my dad, too. Even though he's in Al-Anon and I'm in Alateen, we're not perfect. Sometimes we yell at each other, but at least now we can stop and apologize.

• All these people I love aren't just standing in the surf waving to me—they're drowning! I watch them sinking but they can't be saved unless they reach out for help. I don't know what to do or how to go on, but Alateen shows me the way. Alateens care about me and teach me to care about myself. I learn that I can't save my loved ones by drowning myself. I must face the shore and begin my own life.

Things to Think About

How do I use Alateen to cope with the effects of alcoholism on my family?

What I've learned so far in my study of the Steps in *Twelve Steps and Twelve Traditions for Alateen* is this:

People in the grip of alcoholism cannot make sane, moral, or responsible choices about their behavior or their lives. As a family member or a friend, I am affected by their choices when I try to make their decisions for them. Eventually I'm no longer able  to continue and still maintain my sanity. I have to let go and let God and concentrate on making choices for myself.

Things to Think About

I am powerless over the alcoholic, but I have choices about the way I react to the affected people in my life.

When my father admitted he was an alcoholic, it was a shock. Then the real jolt hit. He was arrested for driving under the influence for the third time and would have to serve time in jail.

After he left, I felt this shadow—sometimes right behind me, or just fading into the dusk. I told lies to cover for his absence and sometimes I just shut the world out and hid, hoping it was a dream. But I knew it wasn't going away; I had to deal with it.

Alateen meetings have saved me. When I'm at meetings, I find people who care about me, people I can't lie to. I don't have to run from my dad's shadow. Alateen gives me the strength to face reality and know that I will be okay. Today I know that I am not responsible for my father's behavior and that I do not have to feel ashamed for what he does. I'm only responsible for what I do.

Things to Think About

"It's easy to hide behind a wall instead of facing my problems, but I'm the one who loses when I do. I close myself in and other people can't reach me. The program helps me to break through my wall and build a bridge to a new way of life."

Alateen—a Day at a Time, p. 228

Getting to a meeting has sometimes been really difficult for me, especially when my parents for-bade me to go because of schoolwork. I didn't know how I was going to get by, but then I realized that there was a whole world on-line that I could use. I'm very lucky that I have a free Internet connection through my school and the public library system. Face-to-face meetings are always better, but when I need a meeting, an on-line meeting helps. I hope I never make the fact that I can't get to a meeting an excuse for not working my program. There is always someone to call and literature to read.

Things to Think About

Have I used all the tools available to me
for my recovery?

I remember the first time I ever saw my dad cry. It was when I asked him to stop drinking. To please me, he stopped. But he didn't do it for himself and eventually I saw him with a beer in his hand again.

One night before Christmas, he and my mom got into a fight because he came home drunk. I could hear them yelling and screaming. I sneaked down the stairs to see what was going on. My dad knocked over the Christmas tree and I ran to my room crying. I laid in bed and prayed for God to help my daddy.

Today in Alateen I pray for God to help me. I know now that I didn't cause it, I can't control it, and I can't cure it. I think to myself my dad has a disease. I ask God to help me make the right decisions in my own recovery from the family disease of alcoholism. This program provides me with ways to deal with the anger inside of me when my dad's disease shows the physical effects. Because of that, today I have sanity.

Things to Think About

Do I ask my Higher Power to help me when I'm in pain?

My father was sober for 15 years when he started drinking again. My parents were constantly battling. They screamed and yelled at each other and couldn't be in the same room without fighting. Finally he moved out, but he kept coming back and leaving again. My dad's behavior hurt, and it made it hard for me to trust anybody.

Meanwhile, I started going to Alateen. Alateen taught me that alcoholism is a family disease and that I'm powerless over it. I learned that I am not the only person who has to deal with it and that feeling sorry for myself just makes it worse. Most important, I learned that I am no longer alone, and I can trust Alateen and my Higher Power to help me.

Things to Think About

"I'm part of a family that's been affected by alcoholism. The best thing I can do for myself is to work the program each day. As I 'get better,' my change of attitude just might help others in my family, including the alcoholic."

Alateen—a Day at a Time, p. 281

Before I came to Alateen, I never understood love. I was a caretaker and an enabler. If you loved me and gave me some atten- tion, I'd do whatever you wanted. I didn't care how much I hurt myself or any- one else as long as you promised to love me. I  caused myself pain and got into tons of trouble, but it just didn't matter.

Since I've been in the program, I've learned that love has no requirements. If you really love me, you will love me for who and what I am. I don't have to try to be someone else or please anyone but me. The better I feel about myself, the less I will need to depend on the opinions of other people.

Things to Think About

My Alateen experience has meaning throughout my whole life; it helps me feel welcome and it helps me love life!

When my adoptive father gave up the bottle and went to treatment, I was in shock. I couldn't see him as anything but a staggering drunk. We both started trying to work a Twelve Step program. I didn't think he could separate himself from the alcohol that kept him going, but he did. I didn't; I acted like he was still drinking. I still wouldn't let my friends come over. I always had an excuse to tell them. One day it came to me that he had changed, and so should I.

Like many people, I have a hard time detaching from anything or anyone that I actually care about. It's so hard to let go. Because of the program, I have accepted his alcoholism, but we're still working on our relationship. It takes time. Through the program, I have learned that I'm not the only one who has a hard time detaching and that if I take it one day at a time, I will be able to let go. Learning to detach with love from other people allows me to place healthy emotional distance between them and me.

Things to Think About

How have I used detachment in my life?

When I went to my first Alateen meeting, I walked into the room and saw two girls I knew from school. I was terrified! I was sure they would tell everybody that my mom was an alcoholic. I wanted to leave, but my brother convinced me to stay. As I sat there, imagining the embarrassment to come, I heard an explanation of anonymity and how important it is to Alateen. I felt such relief because I understood that the girls from school wouldn't tell. My terror and embarrassment went away.

Anonymity allowed me to feel safe. Knowing that what I said wouldn't be repeated gave me a chance to share honestly. I am so grateful that Alateen gave me the chance to learn to trust.

We need to guard anonymity with care. We never know what someone else's situation might be. We want Alateen to always be a safe place where we can share without fear.

Things to Think About

"Anonymity is the spiritual foundation of all our Traditions, ever reminding us to place principles above personalities."

Tradition Twelve

Before I came to Alateen, I was afraid of criticism because of the way my parents used to criticize me. Now that I've been in Alateen for a while, I can accept criticism openly.  It helps me find ways to improve myself. Even negative criticism can help me. First I decide whether it really is a negative characteristic that I need to change. If someone gives criticism out of anger, I can accept the people for who they are and realize they are just angry at the moment.

Today I will listen to criticism from people and say thank you. I will use what I can to help me find ways to improve myself and let go of the rest.

Things to Think About

"I have to stop making excuses if I want to get better. It's not easy, but by looking at myself honestly, I'll be taking a big step toward growing up."

Alateen—a Day at a Time, p. 44

My parents divorced when I was 11, and I held anger and resentment toward my father. Last year I confronted my father about the divorce and told him how I felt. It felt good to finally express my feelings, but it didn't relieve any of the problems between us. In fact, it created more.

At a meeting, a member shared that she had to forgive her mother for what she had done to her. A light bulb turned on in my brain. I also had the power to forgive. I could forgive my father for the pain he caused me. Being in Alateen for seven years, I thought that I understood all the tools of the program, but I was wrong!

It was difficult because it meant letting go of my anger. My stinking thinking changed when I forgave my father, and I was released from my own resentment. Using forgiveness as a tool of my program allowed me to get on with my life and not waste my time expecting apologies.

Although I have forgiven my father, I will not forget what happened in my childhood. My experiences make me who I am today, and I can use them to help others.

Things to Think About

"By releasing resentment, I set myself free."

Courage to Change, p. 289

I've lost many friends in the past. I thought I'd always lose my friends because I was a loser. I withdrew at school and became isolated. I thought it was safer that way and maybe I wouldn't get hurt.

In Alateen I met new people and learned that some people can be trusted, although I had to learn who and how to trust. I began to believe that just because I lost a few friends in the past didn't mean that I would lose all of my friends in the future.

Now I have many friends and I have learned to trust their friendship. They help me with problems and give me strength when I need it. I am learning how to be a friend to myself by listening and being trustworthy.

Things to Think About

"The love and friendship in Alateen can't be found in any ordinary group of teenagers. I feel accepted, needed, and important to other people. Alateens have helped me to turn my life around because they care."

Alateen—a Day at a Time, p. 282

All my life I've waited for a time when I would understand the reasons for my family's problems. I grew up in a home of silence, of unspoken feelings. Both my mother and father are alcoholics—unhappy alcoholics. When I found Alateen three years ago, I felt alone and different from other kids. My entire belief system had been harmed. I was full of pain, guilt, and grief as a result of my family's alcoholism.

There is not a number to measure the distance I have traveled since I found Alateen. I don't know the words to describe the person I have become. In Alateen I found out who I really am. This program has shown me that I have choices. I could stay the way I was, or I could change. It has given me the strength to come out of myself and ask for help.

I have hope and trust in the person I am becoming. I am developing a sense of pride in my ability to change. I can love my parents today without regret. I am nothing short of a miracle.

Things to Think About

"When I live my own life to the utmost, it is easier to let others live theirs. Aliveness is mine. I pray others are blessed with it too."

Courage to Change, p. 348

I often wondered why there were always people in my mother's house—why some mornings I would wake up to find some man sleeping on our couch. These events always involved alcohol. They happened so regularly that it soon became normal to me. But as I grew up, I learned that these things weren't hap- pening to many other families. I felt ashamed of my family.

I'm grateful that my mom real- ized she was suffering from alcoholism, found help, and brought me to Alateen. Very often people don't look for help, and the children continue to suffer.

Alateen is for me, the child of an alcoholic fam- ily, whether my parents are still drinking or not. I may not be able to stop the alcoholic's behavior or help the alcoholic, but I can find help for myself. There are always people out there to help me.

Things to Think About

Do I realize that the behavior of another—no matter how close to me—is not a reflection on me, nor is it my responsibility?

In my Alateen group, we have a few people who talk among themselves, rather than listening to the whole group. It upsets me to see people wasting their opportunity for recovery because I know what that's like.

Listen
and
Learn

I used to do a lot of goofing off myself and I didn't really listen. Eventually I stopped going to my meetings for a while. I thought I knew everything, even though I never really listened. I was wrong! I wound up coming back, and thank God I did. I need Alateen much more than I ever knew.

Now I listen a lot more and I've learned a lot more, too. I never realized how much help I could get from other Alateens until I really listened to what they had to say. When I listen and learn, it really works.

Things to Think About

"The slogan 'Listen and Learn' makes sense when I put it into action. People who listen to others seem to learn the most about putting the program to work in their lives."

Alateen—a Day at a Time, p. 227

When I first came to Alateen, I came because I was told to come. My dad went into treatment for

his alcoholism, and I went to Alateen. At first I hated it and resented having to go. I didn't open up to the program or listen to what people had to say. I only heard myself.

Finally I began to realize that everyone grows at different rates and I was growing slowly. My growth was in proportion to my effort. I was in Alateen for a long time before I actually started living and working the program. Now that I have a sponsor and try to apply the Steps in my life, I have come to understand my feelings and have grown closer to my dad. I love this program for giving me the chance to live life again without all of the chaotic behavior.

Things to Think About

"I have always felt that Alateen is the only place in the world where I can say 'you know' and they know. Alateen is a place where taking and giving are one."

Alateen—Hope for Children of Alcoholics, p. 68

Alateens share on what it was like when they first started going to meetings:

• When I started going to Alateen I didn't like it because, unless it's my idea, I don't usually like doing something. After the first two meetings, I started to like Alateen in spite of myself. I got used to the people and began to understand that I wasn't the only one with this problem.

• Before I came to Alateen, I thought I was the cause of my dad's drinking. Since coming here, I've realized that my dad drinks because he has a disease. Now I know it's not my fault.

• I just started going to Alateen and I feel a lot better now that I can talk about my problems. I don't have to hold them all inside. It makes me feel good to know that I am not the only one who has a problem with alcoholic parents.

Things to Think About

What happened in my first few Alateen meetings that helps me to keep coming back?

About two years ago, I started to transition from Alateen to Al-Anon. Since I graduated from high school, I have been dealing with more adult issues, and Alateen didn't help as much.

I was lucky because I found a good Al-Anon group to attend. It's still awkward at times because I am only 19—and most members are old enough to be my parents, or even my grandparents. However, they learn as much from me as I learn from them. I love them all very much and they help me immensely. I love my Al-Anon meeting.

I realize there are fewer days ahead of me in Alateen than there are behind. I don't need to be afraid to go into an Al-Anon meeting. Al-Anons suffer from the same disease; the only difference is age. If I don't like one Al-Anon meeting, I'll find another one. In this program, we are all the same, and I don't have to do it alone.

Things to Think About

"The nice thing about our program is that it doesn't ask anyone to be perfect, but to keep on trying so that we can feel good about ourselves."

Twelve Steps and Twelve Traditions for Alateen, p. 26

Before I came to Alateen, I was full of anger and resentment. I didn't know what to do with all of it. Alateen showed me how to forgive, give hugs, and call my sponsor. I used to  yell at my sister and I thought I hated her. Now I can give her a hug or say, "I love you."

I'm grateful that my mom is in Al-Anon and my stepdad is in AA, but it's still hard. Sometimes I go to my room and cry. I've learned that it's okay to feel and release my feelings. With the help of Alateen, I'm trying to accept the effects of alcoholism in my family. I read a Step every day, even if I am frustrated or sad. Recovery is a process and it takes time.

Things to Think About

"If I accept alcoholism as an illness today and treat the alcoholic with respect and understanding, I'll be helping myself a lot and that's the best help I can give to the alcoholic."

Alateen—a Day at a Time, p. 172

I came to Alateen because my father is an alcoholic. Although I wasn't in the best of moods when I went to my first Alateen meeting, my spirits lifted as soon as I walked in the door. The Alateens bombarded me with kindness and compliments. The only people who ever gave me compliments before were my family. At first I felt curious about why the Alateens treated me this way, but I knew they meant well.

With all of the meetings I have been to since, I will never forget the first one. After spending five minutes in there, I didn't want to be anywhere else. It gave me a sense of security. I don't know where I'd be today if I didn't have it. I have been in Alateen for several years and have drawn close to the members. The program gives me courage, strength, hope, and it helps me to grow mentally, emotionally, and spiritually.

Things to Think About

"Facing my problems is the first step toward solving them. From this point on I need faith to help me work out a plan of action. If I have faith in my Higher Power and faith in myself, my problems will open the door to a better life."

Alateen—a Day at a Time, p. 292

Life in my alcohol-affected family has been full of depression and anger. When I wasn't angry, I was depressed. I grew up believing that I was responsible for other people's behavior. When they blamed me for what they did, I thought it was true.

Before Alateen I felt guilty for my cousin's death. I felt as though I had killed him and I thought I shouldn't live either. I tried suicide three times, but it didn't work. Now I am very glad it didn't. I know that my Higher Power was taking care of me before I knew how to take care of myself.

Today I am in Alateen, and although I still feel sad about my cousin's death, I no longer feel guilty. I've learned that I am not responsible for other people's choices. I've gained true friends in Alateen and have learned to talk openly about my thoughts and feelings.

Things to Think About

"Anger is only one letter short of danger."

The Forum, December 1995, p. 13

Before I joined Alateen, I had so much anger inside of me and it didn't feel good. I was afraid that if I talked to people, they would judge me. I thought no one would care what I felt and that if my friends found out I went to Alateen, they wouldn't like me anymore.

Eventually I lost my fears and began to believe that I actually did belong. Finally I had found a place where no one judged anyone. It was the greatest feeling in the world.

Now I'm going to leave my home group because we're moving. It's so scary, but I've learned that there will be other groups. I don't have to face my problems alone. I need to look at this as an opportunity to take another step in my program and to share what my group has taught me.

Al-Anon/Alateen is a worldwide fellowship of people who have been affected by alcoholism. I will always qualify to be part of it.

Things to Think About

"Problems aren't roadblocks anymore; they're learning experiences that I can use to help me grow one day at a time."

Alateen—a Day at a Time, p. 292

Lately I've been feeling as if I don't belong anywhere, but when I go to my meetings I fit in. I mean, hey! I have just as much right to be at that meeting as the next person. It doesn't matter about my race, sex, or anything. The only thing that really matters is if a family member or close friend has a problem with alcohol. The person sitting next to me is no better than I am, nor is he any less than I am. Everyone belongs.

No matter where I go, people are about the same. I can try to change myself to fit the situation, but I can't change the people around me. When I feel alone at meetings, I try to look at myself. Maybe something's wrong with my outlook. Thinking positively and really trying to concentrate on the meeting generally makes me feel better. If not, I just keep trying because this too shall pass.

Things to Think About

"Anything and everything about me can be used for my good. If I feel insecure or frightened today, I will remember that my fear is a signal that there is something for me to learn."

Courage to Change, p. 119

Alateens share on what they have gained from the program:

• I always came home from school with a frown on my face. When I got home, things got worse. Now I know that carrying a chip on my shoulder won't solve anything.

• I have found myself becoming more comfortable with the world around me when I share in my meetings.

• Alateen has helped me to concentrate on myself. I've learned to accept my problems as they are and that I am not responsible for other people's behavior.

• When I first came to Alateen, I was scared to talk. I thought that what I had to say wasn't important. I'm still not good at talking, but with the support of my Alateen friends, I know it's okay to say what I'm feeling.

Things to Think About

"In Alateen I learn to change the attitudes that hurt me. There are a lot of things I don't want to do, but making excuses for my actions is just a way of avoiding responsibility."

Alateen—a Day at a Time, p. 209

When I was eight years old, my parents separated. I had to move to another state and live with my grandparents for a while. My grandfather is an alcoholic who was drinking at the time so I lived with active alcoholism for six months. I saw him drink until he got sick and then drink some more. I wondered why anyone would do that. I thought maybe I caused it by living there.

My parents got back together, and I moved home. I'm grateful that I found my way to Alateen and learned how alcoholism had affected my family. Alateen has taught me that alcoholism is a disease and it makes the whole family sick—me included. My sickness was thinking I had to fix things all the time and that I needed to keep everybody happy. Now I try to make my choices based on what I think will be best for me.

Things to Think About

"I will accept others as they are. I will not try to change others, but will try to improve myself."

Alateen's Just for Today

Today is the first day I've admitted that my mother has "fallen off the wagon." I was emptying the trash this morning and found two empty wine bottles. This is not the first time I have found the evidence, but I just didn't want to believe it before. She had been sober for 13 years.

My dad and I will be going to a meeting next week, but that seems so far away. I want to help her, but I know if I try to confront her she will just get angry. I have to use this as an opportunity to start working my program really hard. It was easier with sobriety.

I must go back to the first three Steps. Step One tells me to admit my powerlessness. Step Two reminds me that there is a Power greater than I am, and Step Three asks me to turn my life, including my mother, over to that Power. I know what I have to do, but I need the help of other people in the program in order to do it. Calling my sponsor or another Alateen friend will help me get through this, one day at a time.

Things to Think About

"When I accept the truth about alcoholism, I can do the one thing that really *can* help; love [her] and let go."

Alateen—a Day at a Time, p. 73

I was asked to chair the Alateen meeting at our state convention and was very happy for the opportunity. Conventions are a chance to share with other Alateens and make new friends.

Two days before the convention, my grandfather passed away. I was faced with the decision of whether I should stay at home and fulfill my obligation to my family, or chair the meeting and fulfill my obligation to Alateen.

Grandpa was the alcoholic's father. He died without understanding the disease of alcoholism and spent many days of his life worried about my dad. I was always proud of my grandpa and I know he was proud of me. I decided he would have been proud of me for completing my duties at this convention and for continuing to get help. I chaired the meeting and dedicated my sharing to my grandpa.

Things to Think About

How can the program work in all aspects
of my life?

Before I came to Alateen, I was not content with who I was. I tried to change the way I acted around other people so that they would accept me. I just wanted to fit in. I would act like I was happy on the out-side, but all the while I would feel miserable on the inside.

When I came to Alateen, mem-bers told me that no matter who I am, they would love me. Alateen has taught me the importance of accepting myself before I try to make any changes. If I accept myself, it doesn't matter so much what other people think. Also, by accepting myself, I am learning to accept others.

I can be myself at Alateen without being afraid of being ridiculed. This helps me to be myself in other parts of my life. My true friends are those who accept me for who I am.

Things to Think About

"Liking myself doesn't mean I think I'm the greatest or that I'm better than everybody else. It simply means I'm satisfied with what God has given me."

Alateen—a Day at a Time, p. 298

Alateen is a program to live by and enjoy. My sister had been going to Alateen for about a year before I started. She encouraged me to try it because it 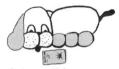 helped her, so I did. As we were on our way to the meeting, my stomach became a knot. I didn't know what it was going to be like or what to say. But when we got there, people were great to me, and after a few meetings, I started feeling comfortable.

I'm grateful today that I have a program. I may not always know what to do in every situation, but I have sources of help—my group, my sponsor, and my friends. I'm learning about the Steps and how to use them in my life. I don't have to know everything today; I just have to be willing.

Things to Think About

"It feels good to be at peace with myself and have enough confidence to extend the hand of friendship to another as it was extended to me when I first came."

Alateen—Hope for Children of Alcoholics, p. 61

When I first came to Alateen, I was afraid people would laugh at me. The more I came, the more

 I realized that we were all there for the same reason. I started to believe in myself without placing myself above everyone else. I'm learning how to work an honest program

using the tools that were freely given to me— tools like acceptance, sharing, listening, and detaching.

Now I love coming to Alateen. It has helped me so much. I don't know what I would have done without it in my life. My sponsor has been the biggest help of all. Alateens loved me when no one else did. They helped me to believe in a Higher Power and taught me what that belief could do for me.

Things to Think About

I want to remember that I am here for the same reason as everybody else. I help myself and others by sharing my experience, strength, and hope.

I suffer from depression. When I finally had to go into the hospital for it, I thought I'd be too embarrassed to tell anybody, but I was wrong. The week I came out of the hospital, I went to my first Alateen meeting. I realized that it was the one place I could share my feelings and my life and not be judged.

I'm not ashamed anymore. Nobody ridicules me or thinks I am some hermit to be avoided. I realize that it's okay to have problems, even serious ones. I know my life has been affected by alcoholism and that I'm not alone.

If there's something wrong, it's okay to tell someone. Most of the time, it just helps to let it out. Now if I need to talk, I know I can count on my Alateen friends to be there—not only to listen, but also to give support. It really does help.

Things to Think About

"The program fills up the empty spaces in my life and gives me a reason to live."

Alateen—a Day at a Time, p. 290

Stopped at a red light with my windows rolled up, my attention went to a woman who seemed totally out of control. Her face contorted in anger as she waved her fists in the air. I couldn't understand what she was saying, but I started to get that old feeling in the pit of my stomach the way I used to with my alcoholic family. Why was I feeling this way? I didn't even know her. I decided to detach by turning my thoughts back to the music and away from her dramatic actions outside my car.

Keeping my car windows up and the radio on were physical forms of detachment. The idea to use detachment came from an Alateen way of thinking. Remembering the first three Steps, I knew I was powerless over that woman. As I drove away, I felt bad for her and reminded myself there was one thing I could do to help her and me. I could say a prayer—something as simple as, "God, let her feel your love today." This is a prayer I said for myself, but saying it might have been uplifting for both of us.

Things to Think About

"No one can make me angry, sad, happy, or anything else without me giving them permission to do so."

Paths to Recovery, p. 13

When I started coming to Alateen, I didn't understand that alcoholism is a disease. I always thought my sister could stop drinking, but she just didn't want to stop. I also thought my mother should stop her. Mother had stopped my brothers and me from doing things we weren't supposed to do. Why couldn't she stop my sister from drinking?

A wesome
L oving
A cceptance
T ruth
E xpectations
E go
N ewomer

After several meetings, I realized I had to accept that my sister was sick and needed a lot of help. It wasn't anybody's fault; it was a disease. I also realized that my family wasn't the only one with this problem. Now I come to meetings every week and feel a lot better. Knowing that I'm not the only one with this problem really helps.

Things to Think About

In what ways do I accept that alcoholism is a disease?

I never knew how important it was to take care of myself until I spent a while in the Alateen program. I used to think it was my obligation to take care of my family and friends. I'd get so busy trying to take care of everyone else that I forgot about myself. After a while, I became so exhausted that I could not physically take care of myself or anyone else.

I felt relieved to hear that my biggest responsibility is me. After hearing slogans like "Keep It Simple" and "First Things First," I came to realize that I was no help to anyone when I wasn't physically or mentally taking care of myself. I know now that I can continue to grow in the program *if* I do what is right for me.

Things to Think About

"I also had to consider why I felt so desperate unless I was helping. When I took a look at my motives, I found that it was my anxiety I didn't want to face."

Courage to Change, p. 18

Before Alateen I remember being sad and scared. I was sad because my dad would come home drunk and be so mean. My mom paid so much attention to my dad that I felt like she for-got about me. My parents used to fight by screaming and yelling. I would wake up scared at night because of their fights. My mom and dad were like monsters to me.

My dad got sober in Alcoholics Anonymous. My mom started going to Al-Anon, and I started going to Alateen. Today we sit down as a family and have meetings together. I'm not afraid of my mom or my dad anymore. My home is quiet and filled with love.

Alateen helps me be a part of this family. Even though my parents have a program, if I didn't have a program I would still feel alone and afraid. Today I have a sponsor and I trust her to help me do the right things. I am so grateful for Alateen!

Things to Think About

"When we have accepted alcoholism as a family disease we realize that everyone in the family deserves our love and understanding."

Alateen—Hope for Children of Alcoholics, p. 36

I always wished for a "father." Don't misunderstand me, I have a dad and I love him, but he wasn't what I thought a father should be. I guess he just didn't meet my expectations.

Alateen has taught me that no one will live up to my expectations. If I keep wanting them to, I am setting myself up for constant disappointment. I need to let go of my expectations and accept my father for who he is.

I can always wish for a better life, but I know that unless I work to make it that way, it'll never happen. Maybe I need to concentrate on improving myself instead of waiting for someone else to change.

Things to Think About

"Acceptance is more than just tolerating other people. It's the kind of attitude that makes me feel good inside. It lets me give people the freedom to be what they really are instead of expecting them to be what I think they should be. When I stop trying to get from people what they can't give me, I can accept them and enjoy all they have to offer."

Alateen—a Day at a Time, p. 137

Today I believe that to live happily, I must believe and trust in a Power greater than myself. I was raised in an alcoholic family and I learned to take on other people's responsibilities. I thought it was my job to fix them and their prob-lems. Who else would do it?

Alateen taught me that I can't fix everything and everybody. Besides, it's not my job! I've learned to let go and let God. When I feel pressured and confused, I can let go and let the power of time take over—God's time, not mine. Time can heal many things, and in the meantime it gives me room to breathe. I'm not God. I'm just myself. I can let the alcoholics in my life go their own way and hope they find healing. By doing this I help myself become a normal teenager who doesn't try to look after everything and everybody.

Things to Think About

"I define my will as the way I'd like things to happen. When I can't have that, I look at it as the will of my Higher Power. I try to remember that the problem in front of me is never as great as the Power behind me."

Twelve Steps and Twelve Traditions for Alateen, p. 10

I thought it couldn't get worse and then it did. My parents' drinking problems were getting out of hand. They just couldn't stop, and on top of that, they were getting a divorce. It made me so mad because I never knew what to expect in my living room at night. I couldn't tell anyone, not even my best friend—it was too embarrassing. I felt separated from the rest of the world.

Then I heard about Alateen. It was comforting to know that I wasn't alone. Alateen has helped me to deal with my anger and fear. I've learned that I don't have to be embarrassed about someone else's behavior; I am only responsible for my own. I've learned that we are all affected by alcoholism because it is a family disease. When one person is an alcoholic, his or her behavior affects everyone else.

Now I work on doing what I can to take care of myself and live one day at a time. It doesn't help anyone else when I worry about the future or am resentful of the past, but it does hurt me.

Things to Think About

How can I use the slogan "One Day at a Time" in my life?

Before Alateen fear was always in my house. Even the dogs would lie down when my dad came in the room. One day someone invited my mom to Al-Anon and told her about Alateen, so she took me along.

I sat outside the meeting and cried because I was too scared to go up to the door. At the first meeting I attended, I saw two close friends. My biggest fear had been that my school friends would find out, and I didn't want anyone to know. Sitting in the meeting, I realized my friends must be there because they needed help, too.

Growth in Alateen is a slow process. I didn't like it at first. I wasn't used to people telling the truth. I stopped going, and my problems just kept getting worse. Finally I came back and cried during the whole meeting. I believe that my Higher Power led me back. My life is good today. I try not to miss a meeting. If I do, I see my old ways coming back. My dad is still sick, but I have to focus on my life. I have to work on helping myself. Alateen keeps my hope alive. Things will get better when I get better.

Things to Think About

"It's hard to act as if everything is okay when it's not. When I keep stuffing my feelings down inside, something has to give and it's usually me."

Alateen—a Day at a Time, p. 243

Prior to Alateen, I was pretty scared when the alcoholic in my family was drinking. She threw things and screamed at me, so I would stay in my  room and cry. The Alateen program helps me deal with my fear. I share all of my feelings with my Alateen group. It helps me feel better after a tough day at school or when I'm feeling sad. I can trust my group today because of the help it has given me in the past.

When I feel bad, I don't take it out on anyone or anything. I call one of my friends in Alateen and tell her what's bothering me. My friend helps me and if something is bothering her, I can always offer my help. I don't do things alone anymore. I let someone help.

Things to Think About

"I have a right to want what I want and to feel the way I feel. I may not choose to act on those feelings or desires, but I won't hide them from myself. They are part of me."

Courage to Change, p. 24

I had a friend that I trusted completely. I could call her and even just cry. One day we got in a fight because I knew she had a big problem and she wouldn't tell me about it. I felt betrayed. We haven't spoken to each other since then, and I'm afraid that I've lost my best friend.

I talked to my sponsor about it. She said maybe once my friend realizes she has lost something as important as our friendship, she'll come back. Maybe I can give her some time.

This situation has taught me a few lessons. Sometimes I need to take the time to appreciate the people around me. If I don't, I might lose what is really important. I am also reminded that I have choices. I can choose to make the first move if I want to restart our friendship.

Things to Think About

"How other people treat me plays a part in how much I trust them. But the way I think can make a big difference, too. When I let go of my past disappointments, I can start to have faith in others and give them another chance to reach me today."

Alateen—a Day at a Time, p. 110

Today I can say I am grateful that my parents
are alcoholics. When I say
that, many people may think
it strange, but really it isn't
strange at all. My parents'
disease allowed me to find
Alateen. Now I'm a stronger
person and I know that I am
someone. Before I didn't know

who I was and I felt empty. Today I have a wonder-
ful program to live by. I'm alive and I know who I am.

I don't have to feel sorry for myself anymore. I
can take what I'm given and work with it. It's like
our sponsor says, "We're the gifted ones." My
Higher Power, whom I choose to call God, has
helped me to understand that.

Things to Think About

" . . . the alcoholic doesn't need my pity and the
non-alcoholic doesn't need my blame. Changing
my attitude can be the first step toward giving
them both what they really need from me—my
love and respect."

Alateen—a Day at a Time, p. 308

Throughout my childhood, my father was an active alcoholic. When he drank, he became crazy. He would beat up my mom and smash our furniture. My mother had five children and an abusive alcoholic husband. She would cry and try to hide her scratches from the night before.

Alateen helped me realize that the crazy man was caused by the disease of alcoholism. Alateen taught me that alcoholism takes control of the person who has the disease. The alcoholic's behavior affects everyone around him. My dad's disease affected my entire family just like a tornado affects a community. Regardless of who gets hurt by the storm, we all have to recover individually and as a family.

Sometimes it's still hard for me to see past my dad's disease—to love him, and to trust him. Alateen has taught me I can recover from this family disease by working my program, one day at a time. If I do, today will be okay. Enough todays stacked together will create a happy life.

Things to Think About

"As I continue to attend meetings, I begin to heal, to find sanity and peace, and to feel much better about myself. I am no longer playing my old role in the alcoholic system, and so the entire family situation begins to change."

Courage to Change, p. 312

My life changed since I came into the program.
I still don't understand how it happened.
Even though I didn't know how to
trust anyone, I found a wonderful, loving sponsor. Warm
and compassionate, my
sponsor always said, "I
love you." I never had to
say it in return. It was the
love that my sponsor had for me that kept me
coming back. For once in my life, I had someone
who loved me unconditionally.

Sponsorship played a big part in my recovery. I
wouldn't be where I am today if it wasn't for my
sponsor being on the other end of the phone. It
was the hope that she gave me that allowed me to
keep hanging on. I believed because she believed.

Looking back over my life, I can see how the loving hand of God has brought many great things
into my life. Now I take the time to feel gratitude.

Things to Think About

"Alateens, in sharing with each other, often find
their own answers."

A Guide for Sponsors of Alateen Groups, p. 3

Living in the disease has brought me a lot of pain. I was overwhelmed for a long time. I felt like I was living in a maze and couldn't find a way out.

When I came to the loving rooms of Alateen, I felt like there was hope for me. I got a sponsor and started working the Steps. One day at a time it started getting easier. It was like God gave me a new pair of glasses. I could see all of those painful experiences as lessons in living.

Alateen has taken me from "life is a maze" to "life is amazing." God has given me the gift of being able to learn from my experiences. I have to remember progress, not perfection, and it gets easier with the very first Step.

Things to Think About

"Step One is a good beginning and the rest of the program will help me take care of myself. I've let situations and other people control me for too long. This is the day I can take control of my own life."

Alateen—a Day at a Time, p. 344

To me Alateen is a safe place where I can express my feelings about my family's problems,

ATTITUDE
OF
GRATITUDE

knowing everyone will listen and no one will laugh. I am never scared to share about anything that's bothering me. This is a real gift because I didn't think any place was safe.

Alateen has helped me to love my parents and myself. I didn't know how to love my parents because I couldn't accept their behavior. I learned the difference between acceptance and approval. I learned that I could love my parents and still not like the way they behave.

Today I can listen to other people sharing and relate to their problems. I can try to help them by sharing what I've learned in the program. Because of Alateen, I have met many new people and have gained many close friends. Gratitude keeps me focused on the positive. When I am feeling down, I will look back to where I was and be grateful.

Things to Think About

"We can think of our lives as books. Each day is a new page. We can make the book interesting or dull, happy or sad. It is up to us."

Alateen—Hope for Children of Alcoholics, p. 55

My favorite tools of the program are the slogans. I use them all the time. My favorite slogan is "Let Go and Let God" because when I have a problem or a situation arises, I can let go of the problem and let God help me through it. When a family member has a problem, I don't make it my problem.

I use "Let Go and Let God" and the Serenity Prayer, because I think they fit together. The Serenity Prayer says, "God, grant me the serenity to accept the things I cannot change, courage to change the things I can, and wisdom to know the difference." I use it by turning the problem over to God so He can help me accept what's happening and give me the courage to change myself.

I use my Higher Power in everyday life because I know He is always there. When I need to talk to another person, I call my sponsor.

Things to Think About

"My Higher Power is a close friend who lives in my heart, whom I can confide in when I feel that the world is coming in on me, someone to laugh with me when I do something crazy."

Alateen Talks Back on Higher Power, p. 10

Coming home after school and walking in the door to find a few empty beer cans lying on the coffee table or on the floor can cause me to be extremely angry. To deal with this anger, I write in my journal. The Serenity Prayer, which is on the first page of my journal, calms me down and lets me focus on how I'm feeling. Then I am able to open  the refrigerator door and reach in to grab my can of soda without noticing the twelve-pack of beer on the bottom shelf. I can also talk to my dad without thinking about how intoxicated he might be.

My daily reader lets me know I'm not alone and gives me the courage to talk to friends about my true feelings. Without the Alateen program, it would be almost impossible for me to be who I really am.

Things to Think About

How have I been able to detach from the alcoholism in my family?

I started coming to Alateen when I was very young. I didn't understand the program, but it felt safe to be there. All I knew was when my parents got drunk, they would hit me and my older sister. As I got older, I began to understand that a disease caused them to do these things.

My parents stopped drinking and started going to AA, and then we moved. I started going to a new Alateen group but the members just goofed around so I stopped going. For a while when something would happen that upset me, I'd read my books and it helped.

One day I was so upset, I knew I couldn't handle it by myself. I went back to Alateen and felt good to know it was still there for me. Now I'm starting over. I'm going to meetings because I need them. I belong to Alateen and I'm grateful.

Things to Think About

"It's easy to be a good member at meetings. But using the program each day is a different story. Taking a daily inventory, with the help of Step Ten, starts me thinking about how much I practice the program."

Alateen—a Day at a Time, p. 152

Both my dad and mom are alcoholic. A couple of years ago, my dad quit drinking and I started going to Alateen. My life has changed so much since I learned the three Cs: I didn't cause it; I can't cure it, and I can't control it. They really help me to let go of little things, focus on what's really important, and get on with my life.

Cause
Cure
Control

Alateen is a great place to go to get my thinking straightened out, but I have to work at it because my problems don't solve themselves. I picked some slogans that had meaning to me and I use them. I study the Steps and try to apply them to my life. Slowly but surely, solving my problems is getting easier—especially when I can remember to turn them over to my Higher Power.

Things to Think About

"It seems easy enough to run away from my problems, but they usually follow me wherever I go. It takes more courage to deal with them face-to-face."

Alateen—a Day at a Time, p. 24

From the time I was four years old, I can remember being told I was worthless. I thought I was the cause of all my mother's and father's problems. As my parents' situation deteriorated, so did my self-esteem. I couldn't find anything to believe in, not even myself.

Then one day a friend brought me to Alateen. There I found that I was not worthless and that I could do anything I put my mind to, with the help of the program and my Higher Power. Through Alateen I found something I could believe in and I found myself.

After hearing I was worthless for so long, it took someone believing in me in order for me to believe in myself. I still have problems with self-esteem, but I know that one day at a time I will recover. Alateen has me on the right track.

Things to Think About

"It's important for me to look at my bad points, but it's just as important for me to look at my good points. It helps me to realize that there is some hope for me and I am encouraged to go on."

Twelve Steps and Twelve Traditions for Alateen, p. 13

At our meeting, we start with the Serenity Prayer. The chairperson reads the opening, and we read the Steps and Traditions. Then we share on a topic of our choice. When I go to Alateen, I listen and learn. One of the things I've learned is that alcoholism is an illness. I didn't know that before. I thought it was just a matter of will.

Recently our topic was anonymity. I listened to everyone share, and I began to understand what anonymity means and why it is important. I realized that it gives me the freedom to say what I need to say without fear.

Sometimes I don't talk at meetings, but even then I get something out of each one. I am very grateful for this program. It helps me to learn more about myself.

Things to Think About

"There are times for talking and times for listening.
The program helps me to sort out
which is which."

Alateen—a Day at a Time, p. 222

"One Day at a Time" was so hard for me at first. As long as I can remember, I have worried about the next day. Was Dad going to pick me up on time so Mom wouldn't get mad? Was Mom going to come home from her boyfriend's house in time to take me to school? Was my aunt going to call the police on Mom when they both got drunk? I didn't know how to live any other way.

After a year in Alateen, I have realized that it is not my responsibility if my parents get in a fight. I don't have to make sure everyone is okay. I have learned in Alateen that it is important for me to take care of myself one day at a time, and I can do that. Taking care of myself is not being selfish. No matter what I think other people may say or do, it's my job to take care of me.

Things to Think About

If people think badly of me because I'm not worrying about their problems, I use a few words of wisdom that I heard at a meeting: "What other people think of me is none of my business."

When I was younger, I hated my father. It seemed like everything I did was wrong and I wanted him to go away or die.

It took a great sponsor and some awesome friends to help me through those times. With their help, I have learned to love my father and become a good son to him. Without the Steps or the Traditions, I would not have come this far. They introduced me to a Higher Power. I have learned how to turn my problems over to my Higher Power, and He helps me through my trials and fears.

No matter what our problems, there are those among us who have had them, too. Sponsors and other Alateens are the biggest help I can get. When I hook up with them and my Higher Power, I can grow.

Things to Think About

"When I really want what the program has to offer, I'll do anything to get it. Going to meetings, sharing my problems with others, working the Steps; all these are part of the new way of life I call Alateen. It's mine today if I'm willing to work for it."

Alateen—a Day at a Time, p. 93

I don't know how to describe the distance I've traveled. Before Alateen my life was completely unmanageable. My problems were overwhelming because I thought it was my job to fix everyone else.

Now I'm in recovery from the family disease of alcoholism. I've had two years in Alateen and I wouldn't take back a day. I feel like I belong and I'm finding out who I really am. I've had difficult things to face, but I've had the support of other Alateens and my sponsor. I feel like God is helping me by working through other people. Recovery is bringing me from a world of pain and fear to a life of hope and love.

Some days I take on too much, and my life becomes unmanageable again. I have to remember, "Keep it Simple." Keeping life manageable for me is about taking things easy, accepting things as they come.

Things to Think About

How do I "Keep It Simple"?

My life was often very hard when my mom was drinking. She did things that were scary and she hurt herself. I felt helpless and alone.

Since I started attending Alateen, I've learned to live with my past and not think about it—by living one day at a time. I asked my fellow Alateens how to accept my past. They said that to accept it, I would have to understand what my past was all about.

By listening to others share and comparing their experiences with my own, I learned what was really going on. Now it doesn't hurt anymore. I accept that my mom has the disease of alcoholism and that it affected my life, too. Sometimes I still have flashbacks, but they're not so scary now that Alateen has helped me understand what is happening.

Things to Think About

"If we try to make each day a good day, we will be paving the way for a good future and will have a lot of good memories when our todays have become yesterdays."

Alateen—Hope for Children of Alcoholics, p. 56

Whenever someone asked me for something, I never hesitated to say yes. I guess you could call me a people-pleaser. I always felt like I didn't fit in, so I tried to give people what they wanted to make them like me. It didn't work! I couldn't understand why they wanted me to do things for them without being my real friends. They were never there for me when I needed them. I learned that they didn't want my friendship. They just wanted me around for what I could give to them.

In Alateen I learned that I don't need to give things to people for them to like me. I just have to be myself. I can't buy friendship or love by giving people the things they want. I can "Let It Begin with Me," by being honest about how I really feel.

Things to Think About

"If we have often been disappointed by an undependable friend, instead of waiting for that person to change, we might try to stop depending on him or her. Perhaps someone else in our life would be more reliable when we really need to count on someone."

How Al-Anon Works, p. 71

Before Alateen my sister and I fought all the time. My little sister knew exactly how to push my buttons and get on my nerves. Then I'd get mad and hurt her, which got me into trouble with my mom. It wasn't worth it. It's easier to stop it at the beginning.

In Alateen I learned to change the buttons that my sister was able to push. I quit reacting to the things that had always worked before. It was boring for her when I used the slogans and didn't react to the things she did, so she stopped.

When anyone pushes my buttons, I can change the buttons. Try it. See? It really works!

Things to Think About

"When I feel like doing what I want instead of what I need to do, I'll remember 'First Things First.' If I take the slogan seriously, it will help me to decide what is important."

Alateen—a Day at a Time, p. 13

When I first came to Alateen, I thought it would help my mother. I didn't like her the way she was, so I wanted to change her. I didn't like my home life either, and I blamed it on her. I had big resentments.

 When I started attending Alateen, my mom was afraid that I would grow to hate her. Instead it taught me to love and accept her. Alateen has helped bring us closer together. Now I accept the fact that she still drinks and I have replaced hate and rage with hugs and kisses, which makes our family healthier.

The program has helped me learn that understanding and acceptance are truly keys to serenity. Resentment is not the key. Neither is denial. I know now that instead of trying to change my mom, I can accept her for who and what she is.

We all have flaws, and nobody's perfect. We can all work to be better people through love, understanding, and caring. It sure beats fighting all the time!

Things to Think About

What has Alateen helped me change?

Alateens share on "Let Go and Let God":

• When I turn my will and my life over to the care of God as I understand Him, I am letting go and letting God.

• My favorite slogan is "Let Go and Let God" because it says to me that no matter what happens, God is always there and He can help me with my problems. I have to be willing to ask and to take responsibility for my actions.

• In Alateen I am learning how to detach with love. This is one of the hardest things that I have to do. I am so used to being a rescuer that I am afraid if I detach from someone I will lose the person forever. The slogan that I use is "Let Go and Let God." It seems to help me the most.

Things to Think About

"My Higher Power is my pilot. My flight through life isn't always going to be smooth. I may encounter storms, but as long as I don't try to grab the controls today, so long as I let Him fly, He can do His job properly and make things easier for me."

Alateen Talks Back on Slogans, p. 11

When I think of how much I have changed in Alateen, it amazes me. I used to be a quiet, shy person who was afraid of talking about my feelings or reaching out for help. Now I'm a person who can take charge of a situation and speak for myself.

People in the program helped me realize that I can accomplish what I want—I'm not bad and worthless. I've learned how to deal with other people, especially the alcoholic in my life. I have learned to speak my mind and to help others with my experience. The main vote of confidence I received was my appointment as representative to our area assembly. I know people trust me now, which is something I never felt before coming to Alateen.

When I'm feeling down and unimportant, I know I can go to my meeting and be appreciated. My group loves me the way I want love from my family. Alateens appreciate me for what I am and who I am—not for what I wear or who my friends are. Deep in my heart I know Alateen has saved my life, and I will be eternally grateful.

Things to Think About

"No one is all bad, and thinking we are is only short-changing ourselves."

Twelve Steps and Twelve Traditions for Alateen, p. 10

I'm not sure where the phrase "perfect family" came from, because I don't think such a thing exists. Some families work better than others, but every family has its disagreements and problems.

My family has to deal with the disease of alcoholism, which can destroy a family. When the alcoholic is drinking, he is not there mentally, emotionally, or physically—but his behavior is there for all to see. Alateen is teaching me how to live with the pain of alcoholism and make the best of it.

No family is perfect but I can do my part in making my family life as pleasant and loving as possible. Understanding the disease and how it affects me has given me acceptance.

Things to Think About

"I've learned that alcoholism isn't something to be ashamed of; it's a disease."

Alateen—a Day at a Time, p. 175

Alateens share on the Serenity Prayer:

• God granted me the serenity to accept the things I could not change when I had to move in with my aunt. God granted me the courage to change the things I can when my friends tried to get me to do drugs and I wouldn't. God granted me the wisdom to know the difference when I was given the ability to make my own decisions.

• I say the Serenity Prayer and try to concentrate on changing the things I can when I react to people and circumstances. I try to avoid worrying about the things I can't change and try to live with them, one day at a time.

• During the day, whenever someone says or does something that hurts me, I automatically want to strike back in anger. Then I stop and say the Serenity Prayer. It always helps me regain my focus. I start thinking of slogans like "How Important Is It?" Soon I realize what a fool I would have made of myself without the prayer.

Things to Think About

How does the Serenity Prayer help me?

My meeting is very important to me. It helped me to open up. It taught me what a Higher Power is and that alcoholism is a very powerful disease. It's not the alcoholics' fault that they have the disease, nor is it my fault that they don't stop drinking. I can't stop people from drinking. I can only love them and let  them go. When they want help, they will reach out and their Higher Power will be there to help them.

I have gratitude because of Alateen. I love everyone at my meetings and they help me a lot. They are my best friends. I'm thankful that they don't laugh when I share and I'm especially grateful that I am no longer alone.

Things to Think About

"Alateen can't 'fix' my family situation, but it can help me to change my attitude toward it. Instead of wishing that things were different, I can accept that things are the way they are and get on with working on my own problems."

Alateen—a Day at a Time, p. 216

I am one of a few students who have joined together to form an Alateen group. We are learning to live our lives one day at a time. Sharing our highs and lows for the week greatly lessens our burdens and gives us the acceptance and fellowship that we need.

Many of us have received help by sharing at the meetings and person-to-person. Talking to someone we trust relieves our anger, confusion, and isolation. To the best of our abilities, we use the Steps and Traditions to guide us to serenity. Even though we sometimes share bad news, we also rejoice at each other's successes and celebrate the anniversary of someone who chose the Alateen group as a saving path.

Our group is open to all students who are affected by alcoholism. We care about each other and try to share our experience, strength, and hope. We're proud that we can make a difference.

Things to Think About

"With the help of Alateen, we can learn to lessen the damaging effect of alcoholism on ourselves and become happy, emotionally healthy people."

Alateen—Hope for Children of Alcoholics, p. 8

Alateens share on the slogans:

• My favorite slogan is "One Day at a Time" because it helps me focus on today's problems. I used to worry about my problems for the next week or the next month. I also like the slogan "Just for Today" because it gives me a daily goal.

• I need to have respect for myself and for others, even when I might not want to. Respect takes practice. It's like "First Things First;" I have to practice respecting myself before I can really respect others.

• I use the slogan "One Day at a Time" every day now. I used to take everything on my shoulders and I would think too far ahead. I became edgy, and any responsibility pressed upon me made me snap. Then I learned to take things one day at a time and I found time for my interests and myself.

Things to Think About

Which slogan has helped me the most?

Sponsorship is fun and challenging. Our group believes strongly in sponsorship, and I want to be there for other people, but I cannot make them want the program.

There was a girl who came to her first meeting and asked me to be her sponsor. Things started off well, and then after we became friends, she stopped working the Steps. She would only call me to do things on weekends. I confronted her about it and she said Alateen was not for her. I thought she really needed the program and it was hard for me to see her fade away.

When newcomers come to Alateen, all I can do is comfort them and make them feel a part of the group. Then, if I sponsor newcomers, I help them when they want it and let them know there will always be a place for them. I cannot make anyone want the program. I can only offer it and help them feel welcome.

Things to Think About

"Sponsorship is a special kind of relationship with a lot of rewards. The best one of all is watching another person grow as he starts to use the Alateen ideas in his life each day."

Alateen—a Day at a Time, p. 287

When I first came to Alateen, I didn't say much and I separated myself from others. Soon I saw  that if I really wanted help, I needed to open up. When I told others what was going on with me, I found it wasn't as bad as I thought. I got involved with service work and became a group representative. Helping at our area conference really opened my eyes. I met Alateens from all over who were just like me. With the friends I made, I felt better. Even though the problems were still with me, I learned new ways to deal with them.

Being a quiet person sitting in a corner is a good way for me to listen. But if I really want to solve my problems, or at least deal with them, I have to talk. Service helps me to open up and gives me a feeling of serenity.

Things to Think About

"Time offers me evidence that the Al-Anon program works—I can see the growth in my life. The longer I live by these principles, the more evidence I have."

Courage to Change, p. 262

I never really knew my Higher Power until I started going to Alateen. I learned how much the disease of alcoholism affected me and I gained the tools to cope with my life as it was. One of those tools was depending on a Power greater than myself. Alateen helped me to want to know my God.

My life had been heading in the wrong direction, but the program and my Higher Power helped turn me around. I need to remember that my Higher Power is in control of my life. If I strengthen my faith in my Higher Power, my life will flourish.

Things to Think About

"Alateen is a spiritual program that gets to the heart of what I need. When I look after my spiritual needs, all other things in my life have a way of taking care of themselves."

Alateen—a Day at a Time, p. 77

Before I came to Alateen, I was always irritated and confused. I wore a mask to hide my true self because I thought I had to think, feel, and act in the way that was expected of me. Eventually I wore out. I was tired of playing pretend and began to hate myself more and more.

Thankfully, that's when I found Alateen, and my life started to make sense. My family's problem had a name—alcoholism. I found I had choices in my thoughts and actions that I didn't know existed. It's necessary for me to have independent ideas and activities. Without them, I drive myself crazy.

Everything started to fall into place, and I began to organize my mind. I realized that I could be happy even when others are unhappy. I had to take off my mask and be true to myself so I could find happiness, sanity, and serenity. Today I believe I am a special person. Alateen taught me to say, "I love me!"

Things to Think About

How does Alateen help you make sense of your life?

The transition from Alateen to Al-Anon is a big step to take. I know because I had to make it when I was 17. I moved to a new city that didn't have any

 Alateen groups. I knew that I needed meetings, so I decided to try an Al-Anon group. I was terrified to enter the meeting. I was afraid that the adults would not accept me, or that they would look down on me. When I entered the group, all of my fears were proven wrong. The Al-Anon members accepted me and were anxious to hear what I had to share.

Al-Anon members accept everyone who has been affected by alcoholism in a relative or friend. Entering an Al-Anon group may be frightening, but once I made that step, I was rewarded with knowing some of the most wonderful people I have ever met.

Things to Think About

"Today I will remember that uncertainty is not a fault but an opportunity."

Courage to Change, p. 69

When I was younger, I thought I was different from everybody else and that no one understood me. I even thought about committing suicide until I came to Alateen and met my best friend.

He told me three things I've never forgotten. The first was that suicide is a permanent answer to a temporary problem. Second, there is no elevator ride to serenity so I need to take it one step at a time. Third and most important, everyone did the best they could at the time.

I have grown a lot since I first came into Alateen and I am happy with my life, even glad I grew up in an alcoholic home. Because of the alcoholism, I had the opportunity to find Alateen and to learn a whole new way of life. It is now my responsibility to reach out to help the new kids who come walking through the door.

Things to Think About

"I am profoundly grateful for laughter and light spirits—and also for anger and fear, because all of these feelings are part of what makes me whole."

Courage to Change, p. 238

Before Alateen I always worried about my dad and what he did. Sometimes I got so caught up in

Homework

him and his problems that it affected my schoolwork. I thought it was my responsibility to worry about him.

When I came to Alateen, one of the first things I learned was the slogan "Let Go and Let God." The more I thought about it, the more I understood what it meant. As I developed trust in God, I knew that it was okay to let go. I needed to turn my attention to things that I could change, like schoolwork.

Spending my life concentrating on what my dad was doing did not help him. The only thing it did was it made me unhappy. Today I will concentrate on myself and what I need to do.

Things to Think About

" . . . 'Let Go and Let God' shows me how to detach and let my Higher Power take care of our family."

Alateen—a Day at a Time, p. 220

As I grew up, I always thought good people had good lives and bad things did not happen to good people. My life was full of bad things because of alcohol. It was only a drink, but it controlled everything in my mom's life. I thought if a drink could control my mom, so could I. I would watch my behavior and my words, hoping that if I were good enough, she would stop drinking. Nothing I did seemed to make any difference, but I kept trying.

By coming to Alateen, I learned that the only person I can change is myself. I lost the belief that I could or should try to change my mom. I know Alateen is my foundation for change. The program is full of helping people who have experienced the same things I have. Alateen allows me to be me.

Things to Think About

"Today I am wiser. I know I cannot harbor resentments and fears. I think this has meant more to my maturing than any other single factor. I owe all this to the Alateen program."

Alateen—Hope for Children of Alcoholics, p. 76

Alateens talk about the importance of sharing:

• Alateen helps me when I have rough times. When I need to talk, I talk to my friends at Alateen. I tell them my troubles and it makes me feel better. I don't share easily because I'm very shy, but I try. I've been here for over a year, but it takes time to learn to trust.

• I like Alateen because I feel free to say what is in my mind and heart. In Alateen I am with kids who have the same problems I do. I can safely share what is going on in my life.

• In Alateen I have learned how hard it is to share my feelings at the meeting. But when I do, it makes me feel better inside. It gives me a better attitude and I don't feel like fighting with my parents. Alateen makes my life happier.

Things to Think About

"Meetings are a time for sharing. When everyone takes part, everyone benefits. If I'm taking up a lot of time talking, I may be hurting others in the group, not to mention myself."

Alateen—a Day at a Time, p. 74

For me the hardest thing to do was to separate my dad from the alcoholism. When I first came to Alateen, I thought people were crazy for telling me that I could love my dad and hate his disease. To me my dad was just a drunk. It seemed as if he were never sober anymore, even in the morning.

Since I've been going to meetings, I've been thinking differently. I've been less angry at my parents—at my dad in particular—even though he continues to drink. I can see the sickness in him because his whole life revolves around alcohol.

I've been trying to take responsibility for my own happiness instead of letting it depend on what others say or think. When I need to talk, I call someone on the phone. I look for the good things in my life so I can share them at my meetings.

Things to Think About

"I realized I was just using my father's drinking as a big excuse because I was afraid to try to change. He was hiding behind the bottle and I was hiding behind him."

Alateen—Hope for Children of Alcoholics, p. 87

My dad was in AA when I was born, but since I don't live with him now, I only get to go to meetings when I visit him. I like my dad's AA meetings, but I like Alateen meetings best because that's where people my own age help each other.

Sometimes it's hard because I am coming and going a lot, but it's easier since I have friends in Alateen. I'm a shy person, but when I'm at Alateen, I feel like I can be myself. I use "Listen and Learn" to help me stay focused. It helps me pay extra attention since I don't get to go to the meetings as much as my Alateen friends. "Listen and Learn" gets my head where my feet are so I can make the most of my meetings.

Things to Think About

"'Listen and Learn': it makes good sense. Using this slogan in my life can help me at home and in school. If I try to pay attention to others, I can learn more about them and myself."

Alateen—a Day at a Time, p. 306

I grew up living scared, wondering when my father would come home and how he was going to act. I remember many nights when I covered my head with my pillow, trying to block out the sound of my parents yelling at each another.

My mind became clouded and I ended up getting myself into more and more trouble. I was put into a juvenile correction facility, which introduced me to Alateen. There I met others with the same problems, but they were learning to deal with their loved ones without letting them control their lives. They already knew how to accept alcoholism as a family disease and they were working on their own growth.

I want what they have, so I plan to find an Alateen meeting close to my home. I want to continue growing and understanding how the problem of alcoholism has affected my life.

Things to Think About

How has living with alcoholism
affected the way I act?

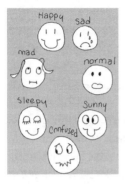

Before I came to Alateen, I was a wreck. I stored up my anger and never let anyone know how I really felt. I believed it was wrong to have bad feelings.

With the help of Alateen, I've found out that it's okay to have all of my feelings— the happy, the sad, the good, and the bad—but it's not healthy to hide them. I've learned that whenever possible, I can express my feelings in a positive way. Talking things out rather than yelling or pouting is hard for me, but with the help and love of my Alateen group, I'm sure I can do it.

Today I'm getting better at showing my feelings. Every now and then I still hide them, and then I remember my goal is progress, not perfection.

Things to Think About

". . . although it's okay for me to feel whatever I'm feeling, I also know when I hang on to those negative feelings I'll continue to suffer from a lot of emotional pain."

Courage to Be Me, p. 163

I was full of anger before I came to Alateen. I hated Mom and I hated my dad's drinking. I used to hide in the closet and try to take care of my sister.

I'm grateful that today my dad is sober in AA and my mom is in Al-Anon. My sister and I go to Alateen. At first I felt so confused that it was hard to tell what I was feeling. When someone asked how I was doing, I usually said I wasn't sure. Now I can really tell how I feel. I know whether I'm happy, sad, or angry. My feelings aren't always pleasant, but today I know they're mine.

**GO ON TO
THE NEXT
AFTER ➡
FINISHING
THE FIRST.**

Things to Think About

"Before Alateen I always thought I was different. Now I realize that I am—in a very positive way. I'm one of God's miracles. There's no one in the world like me. I'm a worthwhile person, filled with good things, ready to make the most of today."

Alateen—a Day at a Time, p. 108

Alateen has changed my life! I always wanted to change my personality and make it like somebody else's. I wanted to stop seeing all the darkness.

Since coming to Alateen, I've begun to see some light at the end of the tunnel, and I believe there is hope. The Twelve Steps are a road map for change that I can use to accept myself for who I am, and then with the help of the program, to change the things I can. All I need to do is pray for courage.

I admitted I was powerless over alcohol. Now it's time to let go and let God handle it. Thanks, God, for my new life.

Things to Think About

"When I discovered that everything is found within myself, I found happiness. Today I forgive myself for all the self-hurt and I promise to give my spirit the relief in receiving spiritual nourishment that Al-Anon offers me."

Having Had a Spiritual Awakening . . ., p. 42

I went to a meeting the other day and heard someone share that he didn't start to work the

Steps for a whole month after he started the program. He made it seem like a month was a long time. I just celebrated two years and I haven't worked any of the Steps yet.

After the meeting, I thought about the differences in the way we were working our programs. I decided that I need to get a sponsor who will help me work the Steps. I can't get anyplace unless I start. I will also continue to use the other tools, like the slogans and the Serenity Prayer.

Everyone has to take it at his or her own pace. I don't need to compare myself to someone else, but I do need to quit procrastinating and start. The program will work if I work at it.

Things to Think About

"I used to think I had to understand each Step perfectly before I moved on to the next one. Now I just keep moving on through the Steps, trying to use them in everything I do so I can keep growing and recovering each day."

Alateen—a Day at a Time, p. 153

Being the daughter of an alcoholic can be extremely stressful. Living with alcoholism stirred up emotions that I didn't have the tools to handle.

Thanks to the help of my Alateen friends, I can honestly say I am well on my way to recovery. I hope one day that these tough times will only be  memories—memories that I can use to help others. I want to look forward to living the rest of my life with confidence and no fear.

Words just cannot express the love I have in my heart for my Alateen family members. They have been there for me from day one. They've never let me down; they've truly saved my life. My Alateen family is my sunshine on rainy days.

Things to Think About

"The great thing about the fellowship is that we can identify with each other. We understand what it's like to live with an alcoholic and somehow the pain isn't as hard to deal with when somebody else knows how we feel."

Alateen—a Day at a Time, p. 98

Living with an alcoholic, I was affected by the disease of alcoholism. Like it says in Step One, my life had become unmanageable.

The Alateen program helped me to understand that I can't rule over alcohol and that trying to do so will make me crazy. When I'm in the middle of such craziness, I have found out that using the Serenity Prayer can restore me to sanity.

Even though I have only been in the program for six months, I have already worked Steps One and Two. I realize that the Twelve Steps are very important. If I continue to work on them, no matter how long it takes, eventually they will help me face all of my problems.

The thing that is most important to me is my Higher Power. I believe that we each have a Higher Power of our own. Alcoholics have a Higher Power, too, whether they know it or not. I know that the Steps have helped me deal with the disease of alcoholism. I believe they can help anyone.

Things to Think About

When I am in the middle of craziness, what tools do I use to restore myself to sanity?

I remember struggling with a family problem. I was obsessed with it! One day I finally turned it over to my Higher Power. I simply said, "God, I can't deal with this anymore. Please help me!" Soon I began noticing a change in my life.

By making a decision to turn my will and my life over to the care of God as I understand Him, I am taking the Third Step. When I think about my family and the things that have happened, I no longer get worried. It's as if God put a stop sign there. The program supplies the wisdom and strength I need to turn my will over to my Higher Power. My Higher Power can help me solve my problems, but the solutions come when I maintain my connection with Him and the Alateen program.

Things to Think About

"The only consistent source of help for matters that are beyond our control is a Power greater than ourselves, and that is where we decide to turn when we take Step Three."

How Al-Anon Works, p. 50

To me "One Day at a Time" means problems come up every day, and I need to take them as

Keep It Simple

they come. I use this and other slogans when I find myself getting all worked up. I repeat them over and over: "Keep It Simple," "One Day at a Time," "Just for Today." I use slogans to keep me focused on the problem in front of me, without worrying about what might happen tomorrow.

When I came to Alateen, I heard the news that I have choices. I can choose to solve problems in many ways and I can ask for help. The best news of all is that I don't have to do it all today.

Things to Think About

"Today is the day that counts, and thanks to the program, I have a great way to make the most of it."

Alateen—a Day at a Time, p. 90

Alateen is a safe place where I can share about myself and relate to other people. I feel like I'm respected for the first time in my life. I hear members share their experience and strength, which gives me permission to share about my life of living with alcoholism.

Alateen helped me to understand that I was powerless over my family situation and that my Higher Power could help me forgive my parents. I learned that I don't have to hold my anger inside. It felt good to be in a safe place where I could share my feelings.

My experiences with my parents are too hard for me to cope with by myself. Now I have the chance to express myself to people who actually care about my feelings. Even when I'm having a bad day, I know I can get everything off my chest by talking with people who understand and respect me.

Things to Think About

"Past experiences, good and bad, are part of the gift I can give to newcomers. They need to know I've been where they are right now. Remembering my past and sharing it is a way to connect with them."

Alateen—a Day at a Time, p. 316

Alateens share on using the tools of the program:

• My Alateen meetings help me to share. I love sharing with others. I read my little red book, *Alateen—a Day at a Time*, every day. At my Alateen meeting, I get to work with newcomers and it feels great. I share my favorite slogans: "Easy Does It" and "Let Go and Let God." If I have a bad attitude, I call my sponsor.

• Before I came to the meetings, my mom and dad used to fight and it was hard to get to sleep. Then my mom and I started going to meetings. Now I have four years in the program. I call my sponsor and share at meetings. I call my friends for help and I use the slogans to help me.

• When I'm mad, I don't want to take my anger out on others. The solution is to use the tools of the program. Tools are things like the slogans, the Steps, the Serenity Prayer, and detachment. There is no reason to take my problems out on others. One day at a time I can look for a better way.

Things to Think About

"Sometimes I think the whole world revolves around me, but the program is there to remind me that it doesn't."

Alateen—a Day at a Time, p. 204

Before I came to Alateen, I always got in fights
with my parents. I'd always say
I was right and they were
wrong. Things got so bad, we
all just quit talking or listening to each other.

Since I have been coming to
Alateen, things are getting
better. I learned the slogan "Listen and Learn,"
which reminds me that I need to be quiet and listen to what other people have to say, before I jump
in with my own ideas. Sometimes I can't wait to
say what I have to say, so I'm not listening to
them at all. I'm so sure they are wrong and I am
right, I want to prove it. Even if they are wrong, I
owe them the courtesy of listening. I've learned to
listen in my meetings. By listening to what everybody else has to say, I'm able to be clearer about
what I think.

Listening is the most important part of com-
municating. My family and I are learning to talk
things out instead of running away from them.

Things to Think About

If I am ready to learn, anyone can be my teacher.

Up until a few years ago, my dad was an active alcoholic. He started going to AA, and then my mom went to Al-Anon. My mom told me about Alateen and how it helps teenagers like me to understand about alcoholism. She asked if I would like to go to a meeting and try it, so I said sure.

After my first meeting, one of the sponsors recommended I go to six meetings before deciding if I liked it. I started to go to the meeting once a week. It has been about two years now, and I am doing much better. I use the slogans and Steps in my life and talk to other members. The best help I get is from going to meetings. I feel as if I'm getting better all the time.

I'm grateful to Alateens for their help and support. I tell all the newcomers to keep coming back. It worked for me.

Things to Think About

"Really listening meant being open to others, being free of my own attitudes."

Having Had a Spiritual Awakening . . ., p. 21

I came to Alateen about a year and a half ago. I've learned a lot since then about coping with my feelings and making my life better. For me the most helpful tools were "One Day at a Time" and the three Cs: I didn't cause it; I can't cure it, and I can't control it.

Before Alateen I would worry about petty little things. Now I've learned to take my life one day at a time and to think about what is happening today. When my mom slips, I know that I can't stop her; she must help herself. If my dad takes a drink, I try to keep my mouth shut and hope he will slow down. If I have feelings that bother me, I can pray about them and put them in God's hands or call my sponsor. I know that my happiness is not dependent on other people's choices.

Things to Think About

What tools can I use to deal with someone else's alcoholism?

Alateen teaches me that I'm not perfect and neither is anyone else. People in Alateen listen to me, no matter what I have to say. I've started to feel a lot better and I'm not as nervous or scared as I used to be. I'm learning to love and to forgive the alcoholics because alcoholism is a family disease. They can't help that they have it any more than I can help how I've been affected.

Alateen keeps me together

Alateen is a great place to find friends and to be myself. Using slogans like "Easy Does It" helps me get through my frustration and pain. I can take my mind off what other people are doing and think about what I am doing. As a result, I feel a whole lot better about myself and about the things going on around me. I've grown and have many more friends. Because of Alateen, I have an overall better life for myself and I get along better with my family.

Things to Think About

"Though no one can go back and make a brand new start, anyone can start from now and make a brand new end."

As We Understood . . ., p. 185

Today I smarted off to my band teacher, and he told me I wasn't allowed to go to my concert or to

a festival this week. The program has taught me to try to control my anger and to take my punishment when I don't. This time I got my punishment not only from my teacher, but also from my parents who grounded me for a week without phone privileges. I even have to go to bed an hour early!

If I didn't have Alateen, I probably would resent my parents big time, but I guess I deserve my punishment. I've learned that I'm responsible for my behavior and that I can't just pass the blame off to someone else.

Before I talk, I need to make sure I think about what I'm saying—or I might find myself in trouble and trying to use the program to deal with the results!

Things to Think About

"I learned a slogan, 'Think' before I speak. I used to just say something without thinking, then get into a heap of trouble."

Alateen Talks Back on Slogans, p. 16

Alateens share on the gifts they have received from Alateen:

• I think Alateen weekend events are a good way for kids and adults to bond and to reach a common understanding about alcoholism. Each gets a chance to see the other's position.

• Whenever I get mad or annoyed at someone, I need to stop and pray. It helps. When I work my program every day, one day at a time, I do better.

• Alateen gives me a chance to make new friends who love me and care about what I do in my daily life. Alateen members are not just there to listen to my problems. They are also eager for me to share the good times.

Things to Think About

"It's a sign of real growth when I stop blaming other people for my 'bad luck' and start doing my part to make things better. The program has the tools to help me do this. It's up to me to use them."

Alateen—a Day at a Time, p. 195

I'm 16 years old and currently in a rehabilitation center for young people with delinquent behaviors. It has been pointed out to me that my parents and grandparents were addicted to alcohol. My counselors decided that Alateen would be a good program for me. It would put me with a group of teens who had the same problems.

Since coming to Alateen, my outlook on my family problems has changed tremendously. I used to feel extremely ashamed of my family. Sometimes I still do, but the program is helping me understand that I have no control over others' actions, only my own. It's also helping me to realize I cannot control what other people think of me. I need to concentrate on what I think of myself.

Being part of a group of people who understand and accept me is giving me the strength to accept myself.

Things to Think About

"Other people keep telling me I'm a worthwhile person. Maybe it's time I started to believe them. Working hard at the program will give me a positive feeling that will help me see the good in myself, too."

Alateen—a Day at a Time, p. 88

D etermination
E asy Does It
T raditions
A cceptance
C ontrol anger
H ope
M eetings
E xpectations
N o criticism
T hink

Last year my mum tried to commit suicide. At this point, I was already in Alateen. She felt that her life couldn't get any worse, so she tried to take matters into her own hands. I wouldn't have been able to get through that experience without Alateen.

In Alateen I learned to detach myself from my mum's drinking. Then I had to learn to detach from her thinking. It was really tough at the start but it gradually became easier. I had to accept that it wasn't my fault that she wanted to die. I was as powerless over my mum's actions as I was over her drinking. Alateen taught me that the best thing I could do for both of us was to concentrate on myself and not obsess about what she might do.

Things to Think About

When I get up in the morning, I tell myself it is going to be a good day. It helps me to set a positive attitude.

My father is the alcoholic in my family. I blamed my mother and my sisters for his drinking. I thought if they would act differently, he wouldn't drink so much. Alateen has helped me understand that he is affected by a disease.

I have learned that I have to face my own problems. If I don't face them, they will not be solved. I can't just ignore them and wait for them to go away. When I told my parents about a serious personal situation, they got mad at me, but then realized that they loved me too much to stay mad. I am grateful that I have learned to face my problems and go on. I can deal with them with the help of my family, my friends, and Alateen.

Things to Think About

"I don't like the obstacles in my life, but often they help make me a stronger person. With the help of the program, I won't be afraid to face my problems today. They'll help me grow and blossom into a better person."

Alateen—a Day at a Time, p. 201

Before I came to Alateen, I was an emotional wreck. I didn't know how to handle my feelings. Either I bottled them up and cried for days or raged, screamed, and blamed everyone else. I've learned to put down the magnifying glass and pick up the mirror.

I've learned to take a deeper look at myself so that I can deal with my own problems. Now instead of blaming, I try to see my part and know that if I really need to cry, I can cry. I no longer bottle up my feelings because that's the easiest way for me to get hurt. Instead I say what I mean, mean what I say, and try not to say it mean.

When my emotions are overwhelming, I take a step back. I try to look at them from a bigger perspective and identify the real problem. If I learn to let go, the Alateen program can show me miracles.

Things to Think About

"Letting go and letting God is a way of achieving peace of mind after we have done everything possible about a particular problem."

Alateen—Hope for Children of Alcoholics, p. 48

The relationship that I had with my mother was horrible. We argued about everything, and I do mean everything. I felt that I had to "win" every argument. I could never be "wrong". As a result, I opened my mouth every time my mother said anything to me.

In the Alateen program, I have learned that I don't have to defend myself all the time and that I can accept criticism without fighting back. Thinking before I speak is an invaluable tool for me. If I can remember that words can't be taken back and that every comment made isn't an attack, I can avoid unnecessary conflict.

Things to Think About

"Criticism can really get to me unless I think it through. If it's false, I don't need to waste my energy getting all upset. If it's true, I can take it to heart and use my program to help change things for the better."

Alateen—a Day at a Time, p. 59

Responsibility was something I avoided at all costs. Whether it was a chore at home, something at school, or anything else that meant I had to take responsibility, I didn't want any part of it. I was always afraid that if I tried something, it wouldn't be good enough or it wouldn't be right, because that's what I was told at home.

In Alateen I've begun to recognize and accept that I can be responsible and that doing so makes me feel better about myself. I can be responsible to my friends by being supportive and available to them. I can be responsible with another member's anonymity. I can be responsible by being a trusted servant and fulfilling commitments.

When I'm willing to accept responsibilities and be accountable, I grow and mature through the process. I may not always be perfectly responsible, but today I'm willing to try new things and learn more about who I can be tomorrow.

If I feel like running away from responsibilities, I will examine my motives and look for an opportunity to grow. I can use my experiences in meetings and with my fellow members to give me the courage to take a risk.

Things to Think About

Three ways I can be responsible today are . . .

My father is an alcoholic. At least once a week he came home drunk and fought with my mom. Finally it became so bad that we left him. My mom started going to Al-Anon and wanted me to go to Alateen.

At first I didn't want to go. I thought, "Why should I go and blab my problems to other people?" But after a while, I started to see changes in my mom and I decided to try it. I'm so grateful that I did because I learned that other people actually have problems as bad as mine and that I'm not alone.

I was wrong when I thought talking about my problems wouldn't help. I've learned that other people have problems, too, and still have a good life. I have choices.

Things to Think About

"The group can be our Higher Power. If we keep an open mind and really listen for new ways to handle our problems, we will find we don't have to be alone."

Alateen—Hope for Children of Alcoholics, p. 13

To me serenity means having peace of mind while everything around me is crazy. Al-Anon and Alateen have shown me things I can do to help myself, things that work for me. I use prayer, meditation, talking it over with a sponsor, and turning it over to my Higher Power.

S elf-control
E xpress feelings
R ecovery
E xperiences shared
N ew beginnings
I nventory
T hings to think about
Y es, I can do it

When I'm upset, I try to get away from other people and be quiet. I may pray about the problem and then try to listen. It helps me to clear my mind so that I can find my part in the situation, because that's the only part I can change.

When I put my serenity first, everyday problems do not seem as intimidating. Just for today, I can focus on myself and not on my problems.

Things to Think About

"In Al-Anon there is no 'right' way to practice prayer and meditation, and—just as importantly— there is no 'wrong' way."

Having Had a Spiritual Awakening . . ., p. 33

I went from a family where I was ostracized and picked on to a program where people reached out to me. I have learned how to be more considerate in my actions and to pay attention to the ways I choose to act and react. I consciously try to accept others because I wish to be accepted. I have stopped surviving and started recovering.

Now as I prepare to move on in my life, I find myself reaching out to newcomers to share the tools of the program with them. I want to leave my mark, but leave it laced with love, compassion, experience, strength, and hope. I need love and compassion in my life in order to accept myself and others. I need experience in order to grow and learn. I need strength so I can endure change and hardship. I need hope so I can survive the lessons that come with change.

Alateen helps me find the strength to accept myself and to seek out an active relationship with the God of my understanding. My involvement with service gives me opportunities to grow and to gain confidence in myself.

Things to Think About

"It takes only one person to start something,
but many others to carry it out."

Lois W., Co-Founder of Al-Anon

When I looked at Step One, it frightened me to think that my life was unmanageable. It sounded like a recipe for craziness. Eventually I found that through studying the Steps my life was not truly unmanageable—it was only unmanageable by me. Actually my Higher Power already manages my life, although I may not always like the way things happen.

Knowing that my Higher Power is in control and believing that things happen for a purpose relieves my fears and even provides me with a little serenity. When things happen that I don't like, I look to see if there is a lesson I can learn and something for which to be grateful.

Things to Think About

"I need to take the First Step again and I'll have to keep taking it for a long time to come. I'm glad about that because now I understand that it's not something I do once and forget about."

Alateen—a Day at a Time, p. 301

Steps Two and Three scare me. They ask me to believe and to make a decision. I can't think of any two things that could be more difficult for me. However, without these Steps, I cannot continue to look for real solutions to my problems.

One day I got up the nerve to talk about my fears at a meeting. The immediate support I received did wonders for my crippled program. The group turned my mountain-sized fears into molehills. Members told me that all I had to do was give my Higher Power a thought when things started to go wrong. They suggested that I spend a moment asking Him for help every morning and thanking Him every night. I've learned that making a decision to believe isn't nearly as hard as I thought.

Things to Think About

"We try to believe the way things turn out will be for our good even if it doesn't seem that way at first."

Alateen—Hope for Children of Alcoholics, p. 14

I am not very religious. In fact, I'm not religious at all. I know that many teens in crisis abandon their religion or God but are afraid to talk about it. It's okay, because I've done that, too.

When I had to talk about "God as we understood Him" at a meeting, I thought the other teens would put me down. I didn't know what that meant to me or even if I believed in it. But they didn't argue with me or try to put me down, and no one hated me.

I am growing fond of the idea of a Higher Power as a system for good, but the great thing about Alateen is that it is *my* Higher Power. I don't expect everyone else to believe in my Higher Power and I don't have to believe in theirs. Alateen is not affiliated with any church or religious belief. We can each have our own Higher Power, and that's okay.

Things to Think About

"Made a decision to turn our will and our lives over to the care of God *as we understood Him*."

Step Three

Once, I had three things to do on the same night. I had to make a decision about which one I was going to attend. It worried me so much that I became sick. Finally I decided to let go and let God. I tried to believe that whatever I decided would be okay, and I was able to think more clearly.

I decided not to attend one event, but I still had to make a decision between the other two. Both were really important to me, and I found myself thinking about them constantly. After another day of stress, I decided to let God have it again. Within 20 minutes, a friend called me and told me that one of the events had been canceled. My huge problem was solved, and I didn't even have to make a decision. It would have been a lot less stressful if I had turned it over long before I did! I am able to feel the spiritual growth of the program each time I practice trusting God.

Things to Think About

How can I take good care of myself while I'm making a decision about something?

Last night my dad moved out for the second time. He is having an affair and wants to be with

 his girlfriend more than he wants to be with my mom and our family. My dad has been drinking since I was 12 or so, and I am used to it. I thought my dad was the greatest guy in the world until I found out about his girlfriend; then I went nuts.

I have to let go of what my dad is doing and put the emphasis back on me. I need to take care of myself by sharing my feelings with other people and by using the slogans and the Steps. I can't change him, but I can change how I react to the way he treats me.

I plan to take care of myself. My dad will have to search for his own source of strength, and I am not it.

Things to Think About

"In Alateen I recover from the inside out. I don't have to hide behind a mask anymore because everyone can see right through me anyway. I can be honest and face up to the truth about myself."

Alateen—a Day at a Time, p. 305

This year I'm going to use the slogans to help me through the hard times. I know when I remember the slogans that I'm putting the emphasis on what I am doing.

• I will take life "One Day at a Time." This is the only day I can do anything about.

• I will "Let Go and Let God." I can't solve all my problems but God can. "Together We Can Make It."

• I will "Live and Let Live." Everything is not my business.

• I will take "First Things First." I won't try to solve problems that have not happened yet.

• I will "Keep It Simple." I don't need to make things any more confusing than they are.

• I will "Listen and Learn." Maybe someone else has a solution to my problem.

The slogans keep me from reacting to other people's behavior. They remind me I have choices. I may not always like my choices, but they are mine to make.

Things to Think About

What Alateen slogan is the most helpful to me?

I have just started my transition into Al-Anon. It's a little scary right now. I have only attended a few meetings, and for most of them I have been sharing as an Alateen. The thing that comforts me is that when I'm in these meetings, I immediately recognize the same acceptance I've found in Alateen. My personal sponsor helps me in my transition by identifying meetings where I might feel most at ease. I am more comfortable with people who are fairly close to my own age.

I do not want to leave Alateen at this point because I am used to it and I have made so many friends. But eventually they will be joining me in Al-Anon, and soon I hope to become an Alateen sponsor. Attending Al-Anon meetings will give me the opportunity to grow so I will have more to share.

Things to Think About

"Fear does not go away because you want it to. But I have learned it can be dealt with in small segments—a day, an hour, a minute, sometimes only for the seconds it takes to say the Serenity Prayer over and over."

As We Understood . . ., p. 205

In Alateen I have learned about trust. If I don't trust others, I will never talk about my problems,

Before Alateen

After

and if I don't talk about my problems, I will never get better. When I have trust, I can forgive. I trust my Alateen sponsors to give me their support. If I trust them, I grow to care about them and to love them.

Once, anonymity was broken in my group, and the trust level dropped. It took a while to get it back. Because of this, we learned how important anonymity is.

Friendship has to do with trust. I trust my Alateen friends as well as friends outside the program. Since I started trusting people, I have really grown. I know our Alateen group has grown for the same reason.

Things to Think About

"The building blocks for respect and trust are courtesy, consideration, and following through on commitments."

Paths to Recovery, p. 330

What is Alateen? Alateen is a Twelve Step program for young people who live in a family that has been affected by alcoholism. We improve our lives by attending weekly meetings where we share our experience, strength, and hope with each other. We develop trust in each other by remembering to keep in confidence what we hear. We learn to believe in a Power greater than ourselves and to build trust in that Power through prayer (talking) and meditation (listening). We learn that to enjoy life we need to live in the present, rather than resenting the past or dreading the future. We improve our relationships with the alcoholics in our lives by practicing detachment—taking care of ourselves and not doing for others what they should do for themselves. Using these principles makes our lives manageable, no matter what is going on with the people around us.

I want to carry the message, not the disease! By working to make my life happier, I am improving the quality of life for everyone around me.

Things to Think About

"Detachment is not caring less, it's caring more for my own serenity."

Alateen Talks Back on Detachment, p. 9

Alateens share on how the program works in their lives:

• I feel like the Alateen program has helped me understand other people and myself. I feel comfortable being with those who deal with the same problems. As the days go by, I grow in my own way and realize new things about myself.

• Alateen helps me get through my problems by talking about them to other people. Everybody in Alateen listens and really tries to help me. It's the only place I know where I can get help. I go every Thursday and I love it.

• When I come home and my dad is drunk, I always remind myself: You can always care about someone, but you can never help someone who doesn't want help.

• When I first came to Alateen, I didn't understand about living. My life was terrible and I was full of anger—which I dealt with by screaming. I've been in the program for four years and my feelings have changed, so my life has changed. I have a second family that loves me unconditionally, even when I'm angry. I thank everyone for being a part of such a great program.

Things to Think About

How does Alateen work in my life?

I used to plan how things would go, always look-ing into the future, not worrying, but expecting. I'd expect things to go badly so I headed into situations with the wrong atti-tude, or I'd expect everything to run smoothly and feel depressed when they didn't.

A sponsor told me that expecta-tions are premeditated disappoint-ments. My Alateen friends told me that I can only be as happy as I make up my mind to be. It didn't sink in right away. Their ideas were just words, catchy sayings. Later, when I needed and looked for help, those catchy sayings looked right back at me.

Now I try my hardest to live in today. I let what may happen tomorrow happen without me plan-ning it. I live "One Day at a Time," and that slogan is not just words to me anymore.

Things to Think About

"Sometimes I have to settle for less than I'd like and be willing to accept it. I won't expect too much of anyone today, not even myself. I'll take it easy and set my goals just a little lower so I can enjoy doing the things I do."

Alateen—a Day at a Time, p. 279

For a long time, I tried to be somebody other than who I am. When I met new people, I immediately started acting to impress them. I think I did this because I didn't accept myself. I started feeling really bad. I thought I was a selfish, unsympathetic person. Then I realized that I had forgotten my true self and I was overlooking the good in me. I was acting, even in front of my dearest friends, and then wondering why I felt so alone when nobody really knew me.

I still feel bad about myself sometimes. I try to remind myself that being who I am is the most important thing I can do. What other people think of me doesn't matter that much; it's what I think of myself that matters. When I have truly accepted my defects, I can slowly start working on removing them.

Today I can save a lot of my energy if I don't use it for acting. I can never be as good at being someone else as I am at being myself. I have everything I need already inside of me.

Things to Think About

"If we hold back and timidly refuse to risk being ourselves, we diminish our relationships."

How Al-Anon Works, p. 96

My mom and dad are alcoholics. When they were going to AA, I was going to Alateen and everything was great for a while. They weren't drinking, and I was beginning to understand that they had a sickness, so I wasn't the cause of their problems.

One weekend I went outside and saw my mom sitting in her car with a six-pack. I thought about running away. I thought, "How could she do this to me?" I told my dad what she was doing, thinking he would try to stop her. Instead, he took a beer for himself! Watching them tore my heart into pieces.

They stopped going to AA meetings, but I still went to Alateen. I could feel myself getting better. It seemed that the better I felt, the worse they became. Finally I had to say something to them because I was sick of it. I told them how I was really feeling and I let go of the results. Eventually they made the decision to stop drinking and to go back to AA. For today our family is doing just fine, and I am very grateful.

Things to Think About

Thanks to Alateen, I learned how to express myself calmly and reasonably, even during difficult situations.

When I first came to Alateen, I used to display my anger wherever I was—at school, at  home, or at my friend's house. Afterward I would feel bad about myself and I really wanted to change.

At my meeting I talked about my anger, and it really helped me to get feedback from other people. They asked me, "Why are you so angry?" Sometimes I wouldn't know, but most of the time I found I was angry at myself because I wasn't measuring up to my own expectations. I learned that it is okay to be angry at myself, but it is healthier to turn my anger into acceptance and to start working on changing the things about myself that I can. Accepting myself for who and where I am today is the beginning of feeling good about myself.

Things to Think About

"Anger has a way of bringing out the worst in me unless I deal with it. Alateen shows me how to be honest about my angry feelings, which helps me channel my feelings into something constructive."

Alateen—a Day at a Time, p. 96

There's a clear blue sky today and it's bright and  sunny. Nearby I see a beautiful rose with a wonderful scent and a bee looking around for pollen.

Before Alateen I was always focused on the negatives and expected the worst. I feared life and I didn't know how to enjoy anything life had to offer. Alateen has taught me not to worry about the negative things. Now I can stand in the sunlight and truly stop to smell the roses. Who knew life could be so good?

Life's little rewards are always right in front of me. It's my job to realize that they're there.

Things to Think About

"Sometimes being restored to sanity by a Power greater than myself means simply accepting moments of spontaneous pleasure that remind me to give thanks for the gift of life."

Having Had a Spiritual Awakening . . ., p. 76

When I was younger, I felt really different from other kids. I had glasses, a buzz cut, and I was sort of fat. I had very few friends, and the friends I did have were not true friends.

About the time I reached the eighth grade, I found my way into Alateen. I made new friends in the program and I even found that I could make people laugh. I realized that I wasn't the loser I thought I was. My new friendships in Alateen helped me to let insults, hatred, and meanness flow off my shoulders.

I'm exactly the way I like me!

Today I am the same person that I used to be on the outside, but I'm totally different on the inside. People respect me for who I am. I don't try to make up stuff about myself to impress them or to justify myself. I don't say one thing and do another. I am totally content with myself.

Things to Think About

"I feel like a different person today—whole and new. I'm free from self-pity and I can carry my head high wherever I go. It feels great and I want to keep it that way."

Alateen—a Day at a Time, p. 219

I blamed the alcoholic for everything that happened in my life. Nothing was ever my fault. One day a good friend of mine pointed out that I need to take responsibility for my actions and stop blaming the alcoholic for my problems. I realized that she was right, but it wasn't easy. It meant I had to look at my part in all of my problems. I could no longer justify my actions by saying the alcoholic made me do it.

Accepting myself as an imperfect human being is helping me to accept the alcoholic. If I can't control myself and do the right thing all the time, how can I expect someone else to?

I'm not changing as fast as I would like, but I'm headed in the right direction. One day at a time, I am learning to be responsible for what I do. Someday I hope to be able to help others the way my friend helped me.

Things to Think About

"I thought, 'Nobody likes me, but I'm a nice guy. I guess they are all messed up.' I didn't realize I was the one who was all messed up."

Alateen—Hope for Children of Alcoholics, p. 85

For a long time, I have taken care of everyone around me. The only person I didn't take care of was me. When I thought I was helping others, I was really hurting myself. Now I'm learning a new way of life. I'm learning that it is acceptable to say no, to set boundaries, and to put my welfare first. I used to think this was selfish. Now I see it as self-love.

Every time I go to an Alateen meeting, I meet people I can relate to. They show me that they care and that I can reach out when I need help. Alateen has shown me that I'm not alone—I'm not the only one with this problem. It helps me and I can see it working in the lives of other kids, too.

The best way to truly help someone else is by taking care of myself. I can't share experience, strength, and hope when I don't have any. By loving myself, I can love others.

Things to Think About

"I came to believe that I could trust myself, God, and my fellow Alateens, and love them freely, without being hurt."

Twelve Steps and Twelve Traditions for Alateen, p. 8

When I first started going to Alateen, I thought I hated my dad. I thought there was no good in him because he was a drunk. All he did was drink, get drunk, come home, and argue with the whole family. I didn't understand that he *had* a problem. I thought he *was* the problem.

Now I have been in the program for three years. I understand that my dad is an alcoholic and that he acts the way he does when he is drunk because the alcohol is in control. The way I act when he is drunk is the effect of his alcoholism on me. Now I know I have choices. Lately he has changed and he doesn't drink so much. I'm grateful, but I know I can't depend on that in the future. I'm thankful that the program has taught me to accept my dad whether he drinks or not.

Things to Think About

"Today I'll live my own life and let others live theirs. I won't be discouraged by what anyone says or does and I won't be influenced by others around me. I'll be my own person."

Alateen—a Day at a Time, p. 212

Alateens share on how their lives have changed since they started Alateen:

• Before Alateen my life was a mess. I didn't get good grades, and everything bothered me. The reason everything was a mess was because I didn't face my problems. I've been coming to Alateen for about a month, and everything has started to turn around. I feel safer now because I can look at my part.

• When I first came to Alateen, if I got mad, I wanted to fight. Now that I've been in Alateen for three years, I am learning new ways to handle problems by working my way through the Steps. Alateen has given me the strength to think about my part of the problem and to move on.

• When I first came to Alateen, I listened to everybody talk and share feelings. I wanted to share, but I thought I didn't have anything to say. The more I listened, the more I understood how much I was like them. Finally I started to share and I began to get even more out of the meeting. I felt great when other people listened and related their problems to mine. Now I'm making friends in Alateen and even getting enough courage to be a speaker.

Things to Think About

How has my life changed since starting Alateen?

In Alateen I have had many pleasant experiences with kids in my meetings, but I have also had a number of misunderstandings. When problems happen, I have learned to talk with the old-timers and then to turn the situation over to God. I stand back, give the person space, and continue to treat him or her as a friend and an equal. It is not easy to do this, but I am finding that it works.

Before the program, I would have been so hurt if I thought someone was mad at me. Sure that it was my fault, I would have tried everything I could think of to help fix the problem. Trying too hard usually made things worse. Today I can look at my part in the problem and then turn the rest over to God. For me this is putting Tradition Twelve to work—by remembering to keep principles above personalities.

TRADITION 12

Things to Think About

"Being happy does not mean living life without a care or always being cheerful. I can be very concerned about things without letting them upset me."

Alateen Talks Back on Higher Power, p. 15

I used to have no idea what the Twelve Concepts of Service meant, but one day at a district meeting we did a workshop on them. That's when I realized how much Concept Four applies to my daily life. "Participation is the key to harmony" not only helps me with my service work, but it also applies to my home.

When I don't participate in the daily events that are going on in my family, things get chaotic. I get angry and then keep resentments. The only way my family life can be harmonious is if I participate. When I do my part, things go smoother and I appreciate everyone more.

When things are not going well at home, I need to look at myself. Today I will be part of the harmony.

Things to Think About

"Participation makes us a part of the group rather than apart from it. Belonging is a deep spiritual need."

Paths to Recovery, p. 270

I recently found out that my sister is going to have a baby. I'm happy because I'll get to be an aunt, but I'm angry and scared because her

 boyfriend is threatening to take the baby away from her. It seems like nothing is ever "normal" in my alcoholic family.

Luckily for me, I have Alateen to help me deal with my reactions to this situation. I am reminded that this is not my problem. I can work on myself and turn my sister over to God. Talking with others and using the slogans will help me support my sister without losing myself in the process.

I can see people who have problems as big or bigger than mine receive help to work through their difficulties. I can trust that God and my friends in Alateen will help me, too.

Things to Think About

"Sometimes the worst 'what if' has to happen before change can come about."

In All Our Affairs, p. 62

I had a hard time at home when my aunts and uncles would get drunk. I knew that the outcome was going to be a fight or at least an argument. While growing up, this was the normal pattern for me.

I found that I needed to make a decision to get help for myself, which was really hard. I decided to start coming to Alateen because I was afraid that I would end up an alcoholic myself. I didn't know exactly what Alateen could do for me, but I was desperate. Alateen has given me a whole new way of looking at life. I've learned that I have choices and that I do not have to make the same choices that my family makes. I'm learning to trust what feels right to me.

There are always going to be times when I have to make difficult decisions. Whenever that time comes, I will talk to another person, think about what's really important, and have confidence in myself to make healthy choices.

Things to Think About

"I can now make decisions about my life and future. All I can say is, 'Thank you.'"

Alateen—Hope for Children of Alcoholics, p. 84

When my father got sober, my older sister decided it was time for her to stop playing the role of mother, so she stopped. I felt that it was my duty to take over for my sister. Alateen has helped me realize that it is not my job in the family to be the mom; it's to be myself. It's not healthy for me or anyone  else if I take over someone else's responsibilities. Even though I think I'm doing the right thing, I'm really not.

I go to Alateen to get help for myself, and that is what I get. I've learned to detach from other people's problems. I'm part of an alcoholic family and I have been affected just like everyone else. I'm not here to save anyone. I'm here to find out who I am and to become the happiest person I can be.

Things to Think About

"Detachment isn't something I only do with the alcoholic. I have to let go of others, too, and let them look after their own lives."

Alateen—a Day at a Time, p. 317

Before Alateen I believed that I was responsible for changing the angry attitudes of people who were hard to get along with. After some time in Alateen meetings and reading the literature, I realized that the only one I am responsible for changing is me. I also understood that I really needed to change, and the sooner the better. As I began to understand the importance of such things as serenity and peace of mind, my relationships at home and school began to change. My problems with the people around me started to clear up.

I don't want to be depressed or angry anymore. I prefer to make the choice that Alateen offers me—I can choose to be happy. I've learned how important it is to quit expecting anything from people. When I quit expecting, I quit setting myself up to be disappointed.

It seems unrealistic to expect that everyone will like me. When I used to expect that, I set myself up to fail and gave myself an excuse to blame the failure on others.

Things to Think About

"When I am disappointed in another's response, I can make an extra effort to be kind, warm, and loving to myself."

Courage to Change, p. 39

All my life, I have exaggerated everything. I spent too much time and energy on my mom's disease, what my friends thought of me, and most important what I thought about myself. I wasted many hours of my life worrying about these things. I didn't know I had any choices until I came to Alateen.

When I first got serious in Alateen and started working my Steps, I learned the four words that now influence my life: "How Important Is It?" This is the most important slogan in my life. Every time I get angry or upset, I can think to myself, "How Important Is It?" and then I know where my priorities stand. It helps me to live more peacefully and to cope with my mother's alcoholism with poise.

Things to Think About

"If I want to make a mountain out of a molehill, I just have to keep throwing more dirt on it."

Alateen—a Day at a Time, p. 309

I never cried at a meeting until I went to my first Alateen convention. Each time I tried to share, I

couldn't finish because I started to cry. I was afraid to cry in front of everyone, but once the tears came, there was no stopping them. Afterward I really didn't know how others would act toward me, but people came up to me and gave me big hugs. After all the tears were through, I felt relieved and I felt loved. I didn't know it before, but I loved them, too, and still do!

It doesn't matter whether I go to an Alateen or an Al-Anon meeting, because there is so much love expressed in the same closing. The phrase "though you may not like all of us, you'll love us in a very special way" is so true! When I take the time to notice it, I realize that we truly do love each other unconditionally.

Things to Think About

In Alateen, what are some of the appropriate ways that we can show how much we care about each other?

Ever since I can remember, there has been fighting, yelling, and screaming in my house. Once I started going to Alateen, I began to understand that my family is not normal and that my stepfather has a disease called alcoholism.

I stopped going to Alateen meetings because I let other things get in the way. I didn't notice how much I needed Alateen. My mom and stepfather got back together because my mother believed he wouldn't drink anymore. She was wrong. That's when I noticed that I really needed Alateen, but still I didn't go. When my stepfather was put in jail, I found myself back at Alateen. This time I knew I needed help.

I need to keep coming back, no matter what my stepfather does. Alateen is about getting recovery for myself and I have to make that my first priority. My family life will never be perfect, but I can get better as I learn to detach from the effects of this disease.

Things to Think About

"When I let my parents 'fight it out' between themselves without getting involved, I find I've got lots of time and energy left over to love them when the fighting is done."

Alateen—a Day at a Time, p. 180

I've been having problems with my friends for the past few weeks. I feel as if they're mad at me. I don't know why and I'm afraid to ask. That is one of the things I've found out about myself. I'm not an open person. I want to talk to other people about my problems, but I'm scared of how they'll react, so I hold back.

I'm really trying to work my program, to overcome my fear, and to risk rejection. I do the best I can do each day and try not to beat up on myself when I fail. Because of Alateen, I believe that in the end things will work out for the best. In the meantime, I can depend on Alateen to support me and love me just as I am.

Things to Think About

"Only by truthfulness and trust can we grow in Alateen. Together, we can make it."

Alateen—Hope for Children of Alcoholics, p. 51

When my dad was drinking, I experienced so many feelings that I became confused. I wondered what was going to happen next, and every night I asked my mom if she thought he was going to be drinking.

In Alateen I learned not to worry about the alcoholic. I need to go on with my own life and let myself love him even when he is drinking. At first I felt sorry for him because of his disease and I would be really sympathetic. Then I got sick of it and became angry. Now I go to Alateen to learn how I can deal with these feelings in healthy ways. By reading Alateen literature and coming to meetings, I can keep a good attitude at home and other places. I listen to other people share their experience with alcoholism and it reminds me that I'm not alone.

Things to Think About

"I not only am, but always was, and always will be powerless over alcoholism. It is a disease. I would be powerless with regard to any other disease."

Twelve Steps and Twelve Traditions for Alateen, p. 7

When I first came to Alateen, I didn't want to be there. For a while, I went to meetings to goof off and have fun. Now I'm growing up and going to

Alateen seriously to work a program.

I feel a lot better since I'm working on me and not the alcoholic or the non-alcoholic. I'm letting God take care of them and I'm putting my focus on myself. I've discovered how much better my life can be when I recognize my part in problems and make choices that are good for me. Taking a personal inventory of myself each time I'm getting off track keeps me going in an orderly direction.

No one can make me change. I have to want to change, and I have my Higher Power to help me. I have to keep working my program so that I can feel good about me.

Things to Think About

"I have got a lot of faults, but there's a lot of good inside me, too. Taking an honest inventory shows me both sides."

Alateen—a Day at a Time, p. 253

I am working on Step Five and I find that it requires a lot of painful self-honesty. I believe God already knows everything I've done wrong, so the hard part is admitting it to myself. Just as the alcoholic in my life justified his behavior, so have I. By lying so many times to cover up, I ended up believing my own excuses. Understanding this about myself has helped me to understand and accept the disease of alcoholism.

STEP FIVE

Now I am able to admit that I have my own problems, things that I never wanted to look at. I can forgive myself and accept myself for who I am. I think once I can admit the nature of my wrongs to another human being, I will be able to go on to Step Six. I'm grateful to this program for teaching me how to be honest with myself.

Things to Think About

"Admitted to God, to ourselves, and to another human being the exact nature of our wrongs."

Step Five

Gratitude is one of my favorite topics. Gratitude reminds me to take time to think about the people and things that I am grateful for. The first people I think about are the alcoholics in my life. If it weren't for them, I would never have found this program or my Alateen friends.

I have a lot of other things to be grateful for, such as family, friends, school, and even simple things like cookies and milk. No matter what it is, the process of making a gratitude list helps me feel better. It's impossible to be grateful and sad at the same time. I try to take a few moments to think of things that I am grateful for each day.

Things to Think About

"Today I will practice gratitude. I will think of some of the things, big or small, for which I am grateful. Maybe I'll even put this list in writing or share it with an Al-Anon friend. Sometimes a tiny action can be a great step toward seeing my life with increasing joy."

Courage to Change, p. 304

I've been in Alateen for one year and seven months. Alateen has really been there for me, especially when my uncle died. I was really close to him.

After he died, my other uncle went back to drinking. I was so scared that I wanted to hold on to him and fix him. I couldn't stop crying for days. I was having a hard time letting go. I went to my meeting, and everyone was so supportive. They helped me through my grief and are helping me to understand what life is like in an alcoholic family.

Thanks to Alateen, I can choose to step out and work on living my own life, basing my choices on what's good for me. I am powerless over other people, even my own family.

Things to Think About

"If I worry about what's going to happen or what's already happened, I'll forget to be thankful for what I have now."

Alateen—a Day at a Time, p. 4

I think happiness is feeling good about myself and having a lot of self-esteem. Happiness involves having a positive attitude and leading a peaceful, serene life. It is being able to laugh and have a good time, and being able to detach from other people's problems.

H
A
P
P
I
N
E
S
S

Happiness is something I can work for in the program if I apply the Serenity Prayer, the Twelve Steps, and the slogans to my daily life. I feel happy when I accept others, look at their good qualities, detach from their problems, and remain optimistic.

Things to Think About

"My life is in a constant state of change. Awareness allows me to keep pace with that change. Today let me listen to my words and watch my actions. Only by knowing the person I am can I create the person I want to become."

Courage to Change, p. 333

My dad is an alcoholic. He gets violent with my mom, sometimes in front of me and my friends. When he does it in front of my friends, I get really angry. I have hated him so much that I tried to run away.

I was told about Alateen, so I went to find out if it could help me. I learned how to talk with other teens about what is going on in my life, and it has made such a difference. Things have not changed with my dad. He still gets drunk, but I've learned how to change my behavior around him and not talk back. I have choices about what I do, but I am powerless over his drinking.

I understand now that we are all affected by the family disease of alcoholism. We didn't ask for it, but it's just there. I need to work on loving my father for who he is and on taking better care of myself.

Things to Think About

Talking about my problems is what it's all about so I can relieve myself of anger, pain, and doubt.

For a long time, I believed the Higher Power that could restore me to sanity had to be the God that my parents believed in. I felt that if I didn't believe in their God, then I couldn't believe in any Higher Power. I couldn't identify with the God of their understanding, so I felt completely alone.

When I came to Alateen, I learned that I didn't have to believe in my parents' God or anybody else's. All I had to believe in was my own. As long as I believe in my Higher Power and trust in His help, He will continue to watch out for me. In fact, He looks out for me even when I'm not trusting.

Things to Think About

How do I show respect if someone else's Higher Power is different from mine?

I've been in Alateen for almost two years, and my favorite slogan is "Listen and Learn." Before Alateen I was constantly playing the victim and

couldn't listen to what anyone was saying to me. I was too scared to face the truth.

Today I believe that my Higher Power speaks to me through other people. When I go to a meeting and really listen to what others are saying, nine times out of ten I learn something that has to do with the problem I'm facing. Since I've been in the program, friends have told me what a wonderful listener I've become. I learn so much more when I don't do all the talking.

Things to Think About

The first time I heard the slogan "Listen and Learn," I thought of it as almost a foreign concept. Now it helps me a great deal to stop concentrating on my sorrows and to really listen to what people have to say to me.

For the longest time, I thought that I was to blame for my father's drinking. If only I had been a better child, if only I hadn't bugged him and asked to go places, if only . . .

In Alateen I learned that I'm not to blame for my father's drinking. It was hard to accept at first, but with some help from fellow Alateen members, I understood. My father's drinking was his problem, not mine. He could only receive help when he became willing to help himself. I do not have to give myself responsibility for other people's behavior—even for those I love.

Some days I forget that I am not to blame. When that happens, I go to my folder with all of my Alateen papers in it and I call an Alateen member for support.

Things to Think About

"Through all of this I know I'm neither perfect nor rotten. I'm somewhere in between and that feels a lot more comfortable than before."

Alateen—a Day at a Time, p. 254

I use the Serenity Prayer a lot, and it keeps me from making so many mistakes. Alcoholism in my family destroyed my ability to trust my parents. I felt like I was lost. I didn't know who I was or where I was going because there was no one showing me the way. Now, because we are a family in recovery, my ability to trust is coming back.

Little by little, Alateen is helping me to discover who I am and to make decisions about where I want to go.

There are others out there like me and that means a lot. I can talk to people in Alateen, and they don't talk at me; they talk to me. They listen and I listen to them. No one tries to tell me how I feel or that I have to feel a certain way. Alateen saved my life! Finding it was the best thing that ever happened to me.

Things to Think About

"Trust is a five–letter word but from it springs many others. If I trust someone, I'm usually honest, open, caring, friendly, respectful, and united with that person. A kind of 'blind faith' runs my emotions, giving me faith in these people."

Alateen Talks Back on Higher Power, p. 29

Recently I was asked to share at a potluck. My grandmother died about a month before, so I knew I was going to have a hard time keeping it together. I was scared to death to be in front of all those people, all looking at me, and waiting for me to say something. As if I wasn't nervous enough, the microphone kept going off. The person next to me started laughing, and finally I started laughing, too. Being able to laugh broke the fear a little and allowed me to calm down.

Sharing that night made me feel stronger inside. My group sponsor was very good at helping me get through it. I was able to share whatever was in my heart and know that I was doing what I was supposed to do. Afterward I felt much better. Facing the fear and doing it anyway makes me feel better about myself.

Things to Think About

"As I stick with Alateen, I learn to laugh at myself. Today I'll find something to laugh about and try to take life just a little less seriously."

Alateen—a Day at a Time, p. 185

Alateens share on the slogan "How Important Is It?":

• When I get frustrated with people or situations, I try to think of the slogan "How Important Is It?" It helps me to calm my mind down enough to get over it. When I think about the slogans, I can have a better day.

Alateen makes me feel happy

• One day my sister and I were fighting over a pen. I read from my daily reader, and it was on "How Important Is It?" It helped me to let go of the pen and to let my sister have it. Now my sister and I share the pen, and we are getting along better.

Things to Think About

"If there's a problem in my life and I caused it, that's tough to face. But it's honest. That helps me work on solving it with the help of the program."

Alateen—a Day at a Time, p. 105

Alateen is a program that reaches out a hand to kids who need help. It goes beneath the skin into the heart, mind, and soul. Those of us who have alcoholism in our family don't always want to talk.

STEP 1

Alateen helps me open my heart to people so I can trust.

I had a hard time accepting that I had a problem, so I can imagine it might be hard for others, too. Alateen helps me learn acceptance gradually, so I can get used to the idea.

When I first came to Alateen I was very hesitant. I mean, who wants to tell stuff to a bunch of strangers? But I opened up at my first meeting because I felt so comfortable. Alateen is a program that helps me to understand acceptance and to change myself, one day at a time.

Things to Think About

How has Alateen helped me to face my feelings and express them?

Lately I've been trying to deal with stress. It seems like I run from one activity to another, wondering when I will get a chance to relax. Every day

 is full, and I can't seem to find time to do what I want to do. If I rush and rush, I start to feel cranky.

By sharing about this problem at my meeting, I learned that I need to take "First Things First." I need to decide what is really important to me. I don't have to say I'll do something just because other people expect me to. There are only 24 hours in a day, and I get to decide what's important enough for me to give it my time. Trying to take on too much makes me crazy, and I end up disappointing myself and everyone else.

Things to Think About

Am I saying yes because I want to do something, or because I worry about what other people will think if I say no?

One day I went outside to hang out with my friends. One of my friends was bike riding with me when he decided to leave and go over to another friend's house. This friend lived out of my neighborhood. I didn't want to be left by myself and I didn't want to act like I needed permission, so I decided I would just go with him. When I got back home, my mom was looking for me. She asked where I had been, and even though I told the truth, I was still punished for breaking the rules.

In Alateen I've learned about pride and how I can let it get me into trouble. When I worry more about what somebody else thinks than about what I know is right, my pride is the problem.

No matter how much peer pressure I get, I need to think before I act.

Things to Think About

"A lot of my problems could be prevented if I'd simply stop and 'Think.' When I feel trouble brewing, I'll use this slogan to keep cool and 'Think' before I act."

Alateen—a Day at a Time, p. 352

Like most people, I came to Alateen because I was at the end of my rope. I was fed up with not being able to control the world and I was sick and tired of losing control of my own reactions to it. I quickly became friends with other Alateens, slowly learning to trust. For the first time, I really felt at home.

When I turned 19 and realized it was time to begin my transition to Al-Anon, I was hesitant about the change. Luckily one of my Alateen friends had just completed his transition. Listening to his story gave me hope, so I attended my first Al-Anon meeting.

To be honest, Al-Anon was a little overwhelming. It was the largest meeting I had ever been to, and the people treated me like I was a newcomer, but something kept me coming back. My trust in God helped me make a conscious decision to keep an open mind about this new part of my life. Soon I got a sponsor and began working through the Steps from a different point in my growth.

Taking the risk gave me so much. I've gained more friends, a personal guide to help me work the Steps, and a closer relationship with my Higher Power. I know that I never have to get to the end of my rope again, as long as I keep an open mind and continue trusting the program.

Things to Think About

Do I feel like it's time for me to try
an Al-Anon meeting?

I have learned that not everyone is in the same spot. I would love for others to know where I am and to understand everything, but that is not possible. The only way they can understand at all is if I tell them.

I know we grow at different times and in different ways. I never understood that until recently. I can see that some of

my friends are where I was a while back and some of them are further along. That is how we can help each other. When one of us has a problem, there is always someone who has been there or is there now. That's why sharing is so important to my recovery. Let it begin with me!

Alateen meetings are for sharing our experience, strength, and hope with one another. Once we recognize our faults, we can ask for help. Eventually we see that others have been where we are, and we are able to share with them. "Together We Can Make It!"

Things to Think About

"If we ask somebody to do us a favor and they forget or let us down, how do we react?"

Alateen—Hope for Children of Alcoholics, p. 51

My life was
kind of like
tic-tac-toe.
I couldn't find
anywhere else to go.

All my life, I saw people fighting, doing drugs, and drinking. When I turned 12, I thought it was okay for me to live that way, too. I started to hang around with my cousins, and that got me into lots of trouble. I ran away, stayed with friends, and ended up in a youth center where people tried to help me change my life. Counselors introduced me to Alateen, which turned out to be a good deal.

I've learned that I can be accepted and loved without having to follow the behavior of my family. My life may be hard, but if I look for help and reach out to Alateen and Al-Anon, it can get better. I know this is true because of the help it has already given me, and I've watched it help lots of others, too. I can love everyone in my family without choosing to follow their example.

Things to Think About

"I realize that while I've been affected by the drinking, I can't blame the alcoholic anymore and make excuses for my poor behavior. I have to look at myself and use the program to become the person I want to be."

Alateen—a Day at a Time, p. 87

My mom drinks almost every night. I hate it! I get so embarrassed when it happens in front of my friends. Many times I've asked myself, "Why?" My mom thinks she drinks because of stress. I know it's because she has a disease.

Alcoholism is an illness. I know she can't control her drinking. I can't cure her and I can't control her, but I can learn to control myself in difficult situations. Whether she drinks or not, Alateen has taught me to love my mom. Thank you, Alateen! I will always be grateful for this program.

Things to Think About

"I want the best for those I love. I am growing to appreciate the joy of fully participating in life. And I choose to allow others to enjoy this sometimes difficult but rewarding blessing of learning from all of their experiences. Today I will live and let live."

Courage to Change, p. 348

When I entered the rooms of Alateen, I was sure I wasn't wanted and that I didn't belong. But once I got used to the meetings, I lost my fear and enjoyed being there. It was such a comfort knowing that I wasn't the only one.

My mom recently had her first birthday in sobriety and I am so proud of her. I'm grateful that I don't have to stay up all hours waiting for her to come home or at least to call. I'm glad that my mom is finally having fun without drinking. The most important thing is I can relax. I no longer have to worry about whether my mom drinks or not. I know that what she does is beyond my control.

I chaired my Alateen meeting for the first time and afterward I felt great. A newcomer came to my meeting, and I could see that he was where I used to be. I got to put my arms around him and say, "It's okay. I was just like you once." Today he's one of my best friends.

Things to Think About

Alateen means friends who will always be there, teaching me to accept when things are wrong and life is unfair.

When I was younger, I wished upon the stars. Every night I'd wish for my mom to stop drinking and to have a "normal" family. I thought if I wished hard enough, my wish would come true.

It wasn't until I found Alateen that I quit waiting for my wishes to happen. Alateen taught me that if I wanted change, I could get busy and do something. After a while, I began to change my actions to fit my needs. Alateen taught me that when I am unhappy with a situation, I can look at myself to see what I can change about my thinking or my behavior that might make the situation better.

Today I accept responsibility for what I need. I still wish upon the stars, but just for fun. I can acknowledge my needs or wants and make an effort to change what I can. Action has become the key to my life.

Things to Think About

"It's a waste of time waiting for other people to make me feel good. My happiness depends on how I think. Today I'll take time to think about the things that make me happy and realize that my happiness is in my own hands."

Alateen—a Day at a Time, p. 142

My parents changed so much. After they went through treatment for their alcoholism and started attending meetings, my brother and I began attending Alateen. What a wonderful support group! Alateen members open their ears and hearts to each other because we have so much experience in common.

For me it was very hard watching people I loved destroy themselves. Nobody wants to see a loved one being hurt, especially by an uncontrollable disease they cannot control. Acceptance is the only thing I could build on.

I am working to develop communication, love, and trust in my family. It will not happen overnight, but if we all work our programs, things continue to get better. Even if everyone doesn't continue to work a program, but I do, I will get better.

Things to Think About

". . . I am incredibly grateful to be alive. I know that my days are filled with blessings, and I cherish each one."

How Al-Anon Works, p. 291

I used to have a hard time letting my mom be herself. I felt like I needed to have total control over my environment, and that meant controlling her, the alcoholic. It was scary to think I didn't have control over what was going to happen.

Step One really helps me. I realize that I am powerless over everything but myself. There are days when I'm even powerless over myself. That means I can let go of the overwhelming burden of being responsible for my mother and everyone else in my life. When I carry the responsibility for myself only, my burden is manageable.

Being in control is not living life to the fullest. Only when I give myself to my Higher Power can I truly live. Step One is a great start on the path to recovery, but I need to do the walking.

Things to Think About

"We admitted we were powerless over alcohol— that our lives had become unmanageable."

Step One

Alateens share on what they've learned in Alateen:

• In Alateen I learned I have the right to protect myself in any situation that threatens my health or well-being, like getting in a car driven by a drunk person or hanging out with someone who treats me badly.

• When I was in trouble and couldn't get to my friends, I'd go to my room and stay by myself. Now I go to Alateen and things get better. I'm learning to control my anger.

• I like Alateen because it helps me to feel better about myself, and I fit in.

• Before I came into these rooms, I was a scared little girl hiding in the corner. I was a girl who desperately wanted to be accepted, but never was because I couldn't accept myself. This program is giving me the life I always wanted—the life I deserve.

• I thought my mother was trying to make up excuses for my father's behavior by telling me that alcoholism is a disease, but she was only trying to help me understand. It really is a deadly disease.

Things to Think About

What have I learned in Alateen recently?

When I came to Alateen two years ago, it was not what I wanted to do. I resented that it took me away from my friends, even for one hour a week. I didn't think there was anything wrong with me, so eventually I quit going.

I learned through my dad's AA program that some of us don't give up until we reach our bottoms. It wasn't until last year that I reached rock bottom and saw how sick I really was. I went back to the group that I rejected two years earlier and was welcomed with open arms. Denial can stand in the way of recovery for both the alcoholic and the family.

Things to Think About

"The alcoholic's family often says one thing and does another. They are not aware that the alcoholic is 'listening' to what they do and not to what they say."

Alateen—Hope for Children of Alcoholics, p. 7

I think detachment means being able to let go and focus on my own problems, not the problems of others. Detachment also means being able to turn problems over to my Higher Power. It means letting go of someone else's problems, but praying for the person at the same time.

Is this really my problem?

I detach by turning my problems over to my Higher Power. I use the slogan "Let Go and Let God" as well as the Serenity Prayer. I remember Step One, which tells me I am powerless over alcohol, and also Step Three, which says I made a decision to turn my will and my life over to the care of my Higher Power.

Things to Think About

"When I stop thinking I have to get involved in everyone else's business, I'll be well on my way to learning how to detach. Then, I'll have a lot more time to concentrate on what really is my business—my own life."

Alateen—a Day at a Time, p. 361

I came to Alateen because my father and step-mother are alcoholics. They are sober today and have been for many years. Just because they are sober, however, doesn't mean the disease is gone or that their actions will not affect me. What they do is not always rational, and I have to remind myself of that. I am powerless over their thinking and their drinking.

I keep coming back to Alateen to learn about the disease of alcoholism and how it affects me. I'm working to accept my parents as they are, not as I would like them to be.

Things to Think About

"The program shows me how to be more patient with myself and that helps me to remember that other people might be 'unfinished,' too."

Alateen—a Day at a Time, p. 293

I once heard an Alateen member say, "Easy Does It, but do it!" This version of our slogan has since become one of my most treasured program tools.

While studying for my school examinations, I have to constantly remind myself to take it easy and not get too worked up and anxious. At the same time, I have to be careful not to relax too much, not to take it too easy. This is something I need to remember all the time, not just during exam fever. Taking it easy helps me to keep my serenity intact, but taking it too easy might bring back the chaos and helplessness into my life. My recovery is about finding the right balance.

The program tools are there to help me keep my serenity. They are not meant as an excuse for avoiding my responsibility.

Things to Think About

"I came into Alateen a year ago, and I would never have believed there was any solution to my problems. There are times when I still feel that way, but it's only because of my laziness. I do know there is a solution and it is up to me to do something about it."

Alateen Talks Back on Higher Power, p. 16

I have been in the Alateen program for about seven months. There are no sober adults in my family, but I have a younger sister and I want her to go to meetings. She won't go because her alcoholic boyfriend doesn't want her to.

Because of Alateen, I am finding myself. I'm learning to use the Steps and the Traditions to help me find inner peace and ways to take care of myself. I'd like to give that to my sister, but I can't. She has to want it for herself, and want it enough to deal with her boyfriend's disapproval. It's hard to accept that I have to watch her go through all the pain and suffering that I've felt, but I am powerless to do it for her. I cannot control my parents' drinking or my sister's thinking. The only control I have is over the way I react to them.

Things to Think About

"I'm still working on being restored to sanity. To me it simply means getting happy with myself."

Alateen—a Day at a Time, p. 273

When I was little, I felt scared to death of my dad. I never knew what he might do next because

 he was drunk most of the time. He used to hit my mom, my brother, and me. One day my mom left my dad. I became less physically afraid, but I was still hurting emotionally. I loved my dad, but I was too scared to tell him. Now that I've started going to Alateen, I am better able to deal with my emotions and problems.

I used to stuff all of my feelings, but I don't have to do that anymore. I can share my feelings with other Alateen members and that helps me to feel lighter and less afraid. They understand because they have the same fears and share what works for them. I am no longer alone.

There are others who have the same problems I do. I need to reach out and be willing to trust someone. "Together We Can Make It," if I am willing to try.

Things to Think About

When was the last time I reached out for help?

Often I feel sad without knowing why. When I think about it, I realize I don't share my feelings, especially when I'm sad. I think it's because when I was little, I always had to be happy. People said that I was a ray of sunshine. I don't remember much from that time, but I think it was like wearing a mask. Even today it's an automatic reaction when someone asks how I feel. I'm likely to answer, "I'm fine," even when I'm not. I don't want to let anyone see that I'm sad because they'll know there is something wrong.

I'm working on accepting my feelings just as they are. If I feel sad, I feel sad. Feelings are okay no matter what they are. The question is, "What am I going to do with these feelings and how can I use them to learn more about myself?" Working Steps Four, Five, and Six helps me to understand my feelings and not be so afraid.

Things to Think About

"If I want to get rid of my defects, I have to stop making excuses and be willing to apply Step Six. When I'm ready, my Higher Power will give me the help I need."

Alateen—a Day at a Time, p. 159

I've been in the program for about a year. Lately I've been getting very frustrated, feeling like the world is out to get me. It's starting to be a constant, everyday situation for me to blow up in somebody's face or mumble things under my breath and just be unreasonably disrespectful.

Last night I went to a spot where I go to gather my thoughts and get in touch with my Higher Power. I prayed about my situation and I feel better, but I'm still angry. I know that the problem is within me. I cannot change my mom, dad, sister, peers, teachers, or other adults, which I keep trying to do. The only one I can change is myself, little by little, one day at a time.

I make gratitude lists, say the slogans and the Serenity Prayer, talk to people, and try to reason things out in a rational manner. My fellow Alateens provide me with wonderful insights from their experience, strength, and hope. Those who make the meeting, "make the meeting." I will keep coming back.

Things to Think About

"We may not have all the answers today. This is not a failure, only a reality."

How Al-Anon Works, p. 68

When my grandmother died, I was heartbroken. I thought my Higher Power had abandoned me. I was at school at the time. During my sixth period class, the lights in the whole building flickered on and off. That's not normal for our school. When I got home, my mother told me when my grandmother died. She died at the same time the lights flickered. Now I feel that she was there saying goodbye to me. I shared this in the next Alateen meeting I attended and someone said this might have been a spiritual experience. It made me realize that my program and Higher Power really work.

Spiritual awakenings don't automatically happen; they are gifts. They happen because my Higher Power is giving me clues about how to work my program.

Things to Think About

"I am a spiritual being having a human experience. I am not a body with a spirit, I am a spirit living in a body."

Having Had a Spiritual Awakening . . ., p. 50

It's still hard for me to accept the fact that my dad is a recovering alcoholic and that my family is affected by alcoholism. I fight with my mother when she finds something I did wrong and yells at me about it. Then my father comes home from work and he yells at me, too.

Before Alateen

After Alateen

I just started going to Alateen but I can already see that it is helping me. When I feel sorry for myself, I do something like go for a walk, write in my diary, or call a friend. Sometimes I just sit down, have a good cry, and start over. Taking a positive action calms me down so I can get things into perspective to deal with my life in a better way. When I say the Serenity Prayer, I am asking for the courage to change the things I can, so I can act rather than react.

Things to Think About

"Alateen gives me two choices: I can hold on to my self-pity, or work it out with the help of the program and my Alateen friends. If I want to grow, the choice is simple."

Alateen—a Day at a Time, p. 196

Before I came to Alateen, I didn't believe in a Higher Power. I thought, "What kind of God would let me get beaten? What kind of God would let me be abused?" Then I stepped inside the rooms of this program and began to listen to others share. By some miracle, I was able to share my own pain. By not giving up on myself, and understanding that I wasn't alone, I began to heal.

Because of the love Alateen gave me, now I can love in return. I no longer carry my pain alone. I believe I have a Higher Power that is with me always. All the bad things that have happened to me have strengthened my spirit. I've survived and will continue to grow one day at a time. When I get into a tough spot, I pray, go to a meeting, and talk to my Alateen friends. This program has helped me believe in God and in myself. The Steps and Traditions give me direction. I have also discovered that being of service to others brings me closer to my Higher Power.

Things to Think About

It only gets better when I let go and let God. When I try to do it my way, things go wrong and chaos takes over.

When I first started going to Alateen, the group I joined was having problems. I wasn't getting anything out of the meetings, so I quit and never wanted to go back.

After about a year, my mom made me go back. When she did, she told me to go just for six weeks. Then if I wanted, she said I could quit. Of course I threw my normal temper tantrum, but by my third meeting I wanted to go back and never stop.

I wanted to hear what people had to say because it was so interesting. That was what got me through my day. They gave me hope—knowing that no matter what I did, I could talk about it without being judged. The group helped me feel accepted and loved.

Things to Think About

"I still have quite a bit to change in myself, but thanks to Alateen, I have made a start."

Alateen—Hope for Children of Alcoholics, p. 74

Fear of humiliation was one of the hardest things for me to let go. I couldn't stand the idea  that people might be talking about me or staring at me because they found out that my mother was an alcoholic.

I felt a lump in my throat and started to shake every time I approached my friends. I just knew what was coming. It wasn't that they teased me, because they didn't. I could just tell by the way they looked at me that they thought I was different from them, but I wasn't. I thought maybe I didn't deserve my friends, and was afraid they felt sorry for me.

When I started coming to Alateen, I found people who accept me for who I am, not as a reflection of my mother's disease. Understanding that alcoholism is a disease has helped me to accept my family situation. I no longer feel ashamed of who I am or of what a member of my family might do.

Things to Think About

"The painful lessons of a lifetime are not unlearned overnight, but [Al-Anon and Alateen are] helping me to learn that it is safe to feel, to hope, even to dream."

Courage to Change, p. 258

When I first came to Alateen, I felt very isolated. I felt like piece of a puzzle that didn't belong to the picture. I just felt left out of everything.

Since I've been coming to Alateen, I have quit feeling so isolated and scared. I've learned that I am not alone and that I can reach out to others. I feel the security of being with peo- ple who are my friends. I trust that they will help me get through what is happening to my family. I must do my part, though, by picking up the phone and going to meetings.

I've also found a connection with the God of my understanding. I've learned how to use prayer to turn over my problems and then to let go and let God handle them.

Things to Think About

"I used to live in my own little prison, locked in by my feelings of hatred and shame. Now I'm free. The key is using the program to do something for me."

Alateen—a Day at a Time, p. 175

All of my life, my father was an alcoholic. He was mentally abusive to my mother and me. I believed that nothing would ever change and that my life was always going to be miserable. 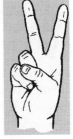 When I was 14 years old, my parents separated and I felt hopeless and afraid.

Finally one day I went to Alateen and found that there is hope. My life can get better, no matter what my father chooses to do. Now my mother and I both go to Al-Anon and I also attend Alateen. I am grateful to have hope. I can see other people's lives improving, and that helps me to believe that my life will get better, too.

I live life one day at a time. Everything cannot go right all the time, but day by day things keep getting better.

Things to Think About

"Whatever is down the road for me does not have to bring fear and anxiety as it did before. Just as important is that I do not have to feel guilt or shame because of what is past. The only thing that counts is TODAY."

Alateen Talks Back on Slogans, p. 28

"We admitted we were powerless over alcohol— that our lives had become unmanageable." At first reading, I thought Step One was easy, but after I thought about it, I realized it was hard. Me, powerless? I don't think so! I have a calendar, a schedule, and I'm pretty well organized. How could my life be unmanageable? At school and at home, I can keep myself under control, but I really have no power over what happens to me. If I don't admit that, I am deceiving myself. The events of my life cannot be managed. I'm powerless over what other people do and how that might impact me tomorrow. The only thing I'm not powerless over is my reaction to what happens.

Things to Think About

"Life is what happens while we're busy
making other plans."

Having Had a Spiritual Awakening . . ., p. 53

Living with alcoholism taught me the true meaning of "Live and Let Live." The alcoholic wanted everyone to take care of him. He decided drinking was more important than taking care of his family—so I thought it was my job to do it, and I did. I even got a full-time job and stopped going to school.

A very special person told me that I was hurting myself and the alcoholic because I wasn't taking care of my own responsibilities. Instead, I was enabling the alcoholic to continue his behavior. At that time, all I could hear was, "If he goes down, my family is going down with him." After being taken out of this situation, I found Alateen and began to realize that alcoholics will do whatever they have to do to support their habit. It is not my responsibility to stop them or to cover for them.

I need to take care of myself first, and then worry about everyone else. I'm no help to anyone if I can't help myself.

Things to Think About

"We have in common the tendency to keep changing ourselves to try to fix something that is not in our power to fix—someone else's alcoholism."

From Survival to Recovery, p. 17

Growing up in an alcoholic home, my idea of love became distorted. My dad wasn't around much and when he was, he was either withdrawn or angry. My mom was around physically, but not emotionally. Her way of showing love was by giving me things or doing things for me. I felt like God was punishing me. Why else did He give me a family like this?

Program people love me exactly as I am. I am so grateful to God for placing me in these rooms. Through the Alateen program, I've learned to look for love from loving people. I've made my own family in these rooms. I can't change the facts of my birth, but I appreciate the opportunity to start over.

Through Al-Anon and Alateen, I've learned that I am worthy, I am lovable, and I deserve unconditional love and respect. My failure to receive what I needed was not because I didn't deserve it; it was because my family didn't have it to give.

Things to Think About

"Sharing my pain was the key to freedom for me."

Alateen—a Day at a Time, p. 10

When I first started coming to Alateen, I thought these meetings were going to be boring. Now that I've been coming for a while, I don't think that way. I like being able to let my feelings out without someone laughing at me. Most members of my group are young, so I feel I can talk to them about almost anything. The topic that I appreciate everyone talking about is anger. I have so much  anger from losing people in my life, but I could never talk about it before.

Since I have been coming to Alateen, little by little I've been letting out more and more of my feelings. Someday they would have all built up and exploded—so I'm going to let them out, a little bit at a time.

Things to Think About

What is a healthy way to let out my anger?

Sometimes I have a big problem with Step One. I love my drinking parent so much that I think my love is enough to stop his drinking. Even though this has been proven wrong time and time again, I still find myself holding on to the hope that this time will be different.

I have to constantly remind myself that I didn't cause it, I can't control it, and I can't cure it. The drinker needs to want to stop and be willing to submit his will to the God of his understanding—and I am not it!

Once in a while I need to sit down and sort things out. I need to detach myself from the drinking and the drinker, take a reality check, and make sure I'm not basing my whole life on someone else.

Things to Think About

". . . Step One means concentrating on myself, not trying to control others."

Alateen—a Day at a Time, p. 198

"One Day at a Time." This is a powerful slogan that members use every day to stay sane and serene, but it also helps people my age cope with their parents. Living in a family with the disease of alcoholism is very difficult. Sometimes the slogan "One Day at a Time" is what gets me through the day. It helps me face my problems and take care of them in a calm manner.

I enjoy being in Alateen with the people who help me. I don't want to lose my temper with them, because they are my good friends. Sometimes I repeat "One Day at a Time" to myself. It helps me to keep my head on straight.

Things to Think About

I try to remember "One Day at a Time" when I think I can't keep going. It helps me when I need it the most. I don't need to worry about tomorrow. If I deal with today, tomorrow will take care of itself.

The first time I heard about Alateen was through a friend. She had been going to meetings for about a year and talked about how they were helping her. I didn't really know what the program was at first.

I thought my friend was sort of strange. Summer came, and she started spending a lot of time at my house. She helped me realize that my living environment wasn't healthy and that I was living with three active alcoholics. She talked me into going to a meeting.

I was terrified the first time I went. I was afraid people would think I was weird. I was so happy and relieved that they accepted me. Everyone was so down-to-earth.

In the meetings I'm learning to share my feelings, even when they're not happy ones. Alateen has given me some of the most important relationships in my life. Sometimes when I'm feeling bad, the thing that keeps me coming back is the people. They are my connection to a better life.

Things to Think About

I don't need to be afraid to say what I feel. I never know what someone else may need to hear.

I've learned to find the good in bad situations. When my dad died, I was very hurt and upset, but I knew God was in control. I realized God took my father out of this world where there was so much pain and misery in his life. I have no idea what my dad thought of all the pain he endured. I'm grateful that his suffering is over. Most of all, I'm glad that I had eight years in this  program to focus on myself, instead of on my dad. I put my energy into improving myself in the hope that I can be a living example for other Alateens.

I have no idea how great other people's pain is. I can't know all they've been through and how it has affected them. It's not up to me to judge others' behavior either, but to look for the positive wherever I can find it.

Things to Think About

"If I look for the good in something instead of the bad, I'm much happier."

Alateen—a Day at a Time, p. 193

My friend and I have parents who are alcoholics. When we heard about Alateen, we thought we

Take me to Alateen quick!

would go one time. At our first meeting, we learned that we were powerless over alcoholism, that we weren't alone, and that other teens had the same kinds of problems that we had. When we got home that day, my friend and I talked and decided we wanted to give the program a try.

Before Alateen I thought I was responsible for what my parents were doing. Now I know that I didn't cause it and that I can't control or cure the alcoholism in my family. I use the slogans and read every day from my Alateen literature to keep myself sane. I go back every week because I know I need help and my Alateen group is willing to give it to me.

Things to Think About

"I know now that when problems happen in my life, whether I realize it at the time or not, everything will turn out for the best for me because God is taking care of my life and His will is being carried out."

Alateen Talks Back on Higher Power, p. 15

My Alateen meeting is great. I have learned that I am not alone and I am no different from other kids who suffer from the family disease of alcoholism. It's nice to know that there are Alateen meetings where people can help me by sharing their experiences, and I can help others by sharing mine. This helps me to grow and to feel good about myself.

When I first came to Alateen, I was scared that I would not fit in with the other kids. I had usually felt like a square peg trying to fit into a round hole. In Alateen people were caring and understanding. I didn't have to match anyone's expectations in order to fit in. Everybody shared with each other, and I thought it was great.

I'm grateful for the love and support that I have found in Alateen. Today I try to reach out to newcomers the way other members reached out to me.

Things to Think About

"Reaching out is caring for others and myself in a special way. Today I'll reach out and let myself get close to people."

Alateen—a Day at a Time, p. 19

I'm in Alateen because I have an alcoholic aunt. Even when I was little, I could tell there was something wrong in my family.

Once on my aunt's birthday, I got really uncomfortable and scared. We were at a restaurant, and she started acting funny. I felt like she was staring at me while she was knocking things over on the table. It didn't seem like anyone was having a good time. She couldn't drive, and someone else had to take us home. Nobody in my family said anything about what was going on.

I found out later that she acted that way because she was sick and had a disease called alcoholism. My family denied that she had a problem. That's why everybody acted so strange. I still love her and I need to be around her, but she scares me.

I use the Serenity Prayer when I have to be around my aunt. I ask, "God, grant me the serenity to accept the things I cannot change, courage to change the things I can, and wisdom to know the difference."

Things to Think About

"In Alateen, when we say alcoholism is a family disease, we mean that the alcoholism of one member affects the whole family, and all become sick."

Alateen—Hope for Children of Alcoholics, p. 6

Some days I go to school scared about what will happen that day. I may have problems in  school or things that I'm afraid to talk about with the alcoholic. I can talk to Alateens about my fears, and that helps me.

Fear is something I don't want, but I must deal with it and not let it overwhelm me. I've been told fear is "false evidence appearing real." Being afraid is not wrong, because it is perfectly normal. It can be a real learning experience to face my fear and walk through it. Fear can be one of the best tools in dealing with my problems. Once I've recognized that my problem is caused by fear, the battle is halfway won. Facing my fear can make me a strong-minded individual. It can be my secret weapon in our ever-changing world.

Things to Think About

"Today I can admit that I'm afraid. There's nothing wrong with that. I'm learning to identify my fears and face them."

Alateen—a Day at a Time, p. 223

Recently I had softball tryouts. I was so scared that I messed up at base running. I went home and cried, but I kept quiet about it because I didn't want to bring attention to myself. For years my father ruled the house. I had to stay low and not upset him. I learned to hide my fears so I wouldn't get picked on.

I tried out for softball again. This time my batting was horrible, so I went home upset again, but this time I called my friend. He told me that if you don't think you can do it, you won't be able to.

As I sat there and thought about what he said, Step One came into my mind. I was powerless at being the best, but I could still do my best and that was good enough. At the final tryout, I stood there shaking but I swung the bat with all my heart. That night I went home calm. I was powerless over the judge's decision, but I was satisfied that I'd done my best. The next day, I ran to the field house and saw my name on the list. I was overjoyed, but it was like icing on a cake. It made it better, but it would have been good anyway.

Things to Think About

"Whatever I'm doing, I'm inclined to feel that I'm doing it wrong, that my best is not good enough. And that is simply not true. I am doing just fine."

Courage to Change, p. 255

I've learned that I'm powerless over alcohol. I've admitted that I can't do anything to fix the alcoholic, but sometimes I find myself wondering if I should do something. I have to remind myself that sometimes my helping can make things worse. I can't change another person's actions or feelings, but I can change my reactions to them.

I've also accepted the fact that my stepfather is an alcoholic. I know it will take time before things get better. I used to get so angry and scared when he yelled at me that I would run to my room and cry my eyes out. Now, thanks to Alateen, instead of absorbing his words, I can let them roll off while I focus on more important things.

I like Alateen a lot. It is helping me to be a better person. Other Alateen members have experienced some of the same situations, and they understand. I love having people in my life who will really listen to what I have to say.

Things to Think About

"Alateen helps me understand alcoholism. But it doesn't stop there. It's a program of living that can help me understand myself and gives a sense of direction to every part of my life."

Alateen—a Day at a Time, p. 94

The transition from Alateen to Al-Anon has been a long, scary process for me. I've been in the program of Alateen for seven years and I've been attending Al-Anon for close to a year. The truth is, I'm not scared of Al-Anon but I'm afraid of losing my friends.

The Alateen program has been the backbone of my life for a long time, and it's always been exactly what I needed to get through the hard times. Part of me was afraid that I wouldn't find what I need in Al-Anon. Since I've started attending Al-Anon meetings, I realize that they contain all the love, growth, and tools of the program that I've come to know in Alateen.

It's scary, but it's good to know that I will still have someplace to go when Alateen is no longer an option.

Things to Think About

"Sometimes it's hard to think about moving from Alateen to Al-Anon.. . . When I'm ready to move on, I won't be leaving my Alateen friends behind; I'll just be getting to know another group of friends who can help me grow up and get what I need out of the program."

Alateen—a Day at a Time, p. 246

Alateen has made me aware that reacting to someone's behavior is a choice. The difference between acting and reacting is the thinking involved.

When I react, I do things based purely on circumstances outside my control. Very rarely do I think through what I do before I do it. When I act, I consider my options and do what is best for me.

Go one step at a time.

1. Think.
2. Easy does it
3. One day at a time
4. Keep it simple
5. Listen and Learn
6. Live and let Live
7. First things First
8. How important is it?
9. Together we can make it.
10. Let go and Let god

Slogans like "Think" allow me to take my time before acting. Sometimes all I need to do to make better decisions is take a deep breath and get in the right train of thought. A slogan is a reminder that I have choices.

Things to Think About

What do I use to remind me to stop and think before I react?

I was raised in an alcoholic family and had been a member of the Alateen program for three years when I entered an abusive relationship. I began feeling stupid and worthless. I believed everything he said and I hated myself. I didn't feel that I had the choice of leaving or staying. He said that I couldn't leave, so I didn't.

I stayed in the relationship for about five months, but continued going to occasional Alateen meetings. One night I heard in a meeting that I had choices! I decided to make a choice and leave the relationship. It was very hard following through on my decision, but with the support of the people in the program, I was successful.

I realize today that it is easy for me to fall into a bad relationship because poor relationships seemed normal in my childhood. I didn't learn to feel good enough about myself to refuse abusive behavior. Today my life is getting better, and as Alateens say, I'm taking it one day at a time.

Things to Think About

"Today I'm free from my past mistakes. Instead of making the same ones over and over again, I can learn from them so I don't have to repeat them."

Alateen—a Day at a Time, p. 295

I remember when I first started my "new life." I was full of resentment because I felt alcoholism had robbed me of my childhood fun. At the age of 16, I was going to school, holding down a full-time job, and providing my family's only source of income. My past was a good reason to feel sorry for myself and to stay in the victim role.

Eventually, through my sponsor and my Higher Power whom I call God, I realized that I was making a choice to do these things and that everybody in my family was doing the best he or she could.

Today I still visit the past, but I no longer want to live there. I always come back to today.

Things to Think About

"When I stop feeling sorry for myself and start working the program, I get a new outlook on life. The obstacles in front of me don't look so big if I use the Steps, the slogans, and the Serenity Prayer to deal with them."

Alateen—a Day at a Time, p. 35

I didn't think anyone had problems as bad as mine, until I came to Alateen. Thinking that way gave me plenty of reasons to feel sorry for myself. As I attended more meetings, my eyes started to open. Some people's problems made mine look small, but they were facing them with courage. Other people were in situations as bad as mine, but they didn't act as though it was the end of the world. They accepted the fact that the alcoholic in their life was suffering from a disease and started doing something about themselves.

Now I use the program to work on my own problems. I know there are no easy solutions, but facing them and working through them is a lot better than turning my back and feeling sorry for myself.

Self-pity is a problem, not a solution. Other kids have troubles, too, but they aren't sitting around feeling sorry for themselves. They use the program to change their reaction to their problems. It's time I did something about mine.

Things to Think About

"There are still times when I hurt inside. Other people can make me feel good for awhile, but I have to do something for myself if I really want to get rid of the pain."

Alateen—a Day at a Time, p. 182

One thing I used to take away from my Alateen meeting every week was a sense of peace—a feeling that even if something doesn't get done right now, it will be okay. My group disintegrated, and I lost that sense of serenity for a while. Lately I'm finding myself in a rat race and I'm reaching for inner peace again. Alateen taught me where to find it, so I need to find another meeting and make it my home group. Alateen connects me to God, and God gives me inner peace.

Sometimes I've been asked, "Have you made your peace with your God?" I answer that I've never quarreled with my God, but sometimes I have turned my back and wandered away.

Things to Think About

"Serenity may be the most precious gift we receive because it allows us to know that our lives are in the care of a Power greater than ourselves and therefore, even in the midst of chaos, there is hope."

How Al-Anon Works, p. 82

When the group representative (GR) commitment came up in my Alateen meeting, I volunteered without knowing how much it was going to help me grow. At first I was nervous because I didn't know much about service work. The Al-Anons at the district and area meetings welcomed me and seemed excited to have an Alateen attend. It was my responsibility to be the voice and vote for my Alateen meeting.

Being the group representative helped tremendously with my transition into Al-Anon! I got to know the other Al-Anons in my area. It set a foundation of service for my transition. I learned about the Concepts of Service and the service structure of Al-Anon. The most important thing was that I felt a part of Al-Anon Family Groups.

I never know what gifts will come out of service work. If I am just willing, God will take me down a path that is beyond my dreams. Today I will be willing to be of service to Alateen.

Things to Think About

"A GR is a vital link in the continuing function, growth, and unity of world Al-Anon."

Al-Anon/Alateen Service Manual, p. 126

One year ago today was my first Alateen meeting. This is a special day for me.

I've had help for a year and I'm no longer afraid to bring my friends home because my dad might be drunk. Today I know that I'm not responsible for my dad's behavior. I don't have to be embarrassed or ashamed of anyone's behavior but my own. My year of coming to Alateen has made me a stronger person.

The fear, shame, and guilt that I constantly struggled with have been replaced by courage, acceptance, and freedom that enable me to live, rather than just survive.

Things to Think About

"Just as I cannot live anyone's life for them, no one can live mine for me."

Paths to Recovery, p. 200

The simple fact is that no one, absolutely no one, understands an Alateen like another Alateen. By sharing experience, strength, hope, and understanding, we are all hooked together through a common problem. In sharing my brokenness with someone in my group who will listen and care, I begin to heal. It's only through  giving away what I have that I am able to keep it. Most important, there is one who presides over us all, one that is in charge of the group, and that one is God. The more I come back and share, the closer I get to my Higher Power.

Let me be of maximum service to my Higher Power today by being of service to my fellow man. Let me pray for the courage and the strength to be open with my fellow Alateens. Allow me to remember to rely on the only authority in the group.

Things to Think About

Today I will be grateful to be alive and I'll celebrate the joy of life.

I went to Alateen thinking that I could help my brother overcome alcoholism. I soon realized that only he could help himself. I learned that alco-  holism is a family disease and that my need to save everybody was part of my sickness. By going to Alateen, I am giving myself a chance to recover.

My Alateen group helped me through some really tough times and still helps me today. When anything starts to bother me, I can remember the slogans "One Day at a Time" and "Let Go and Let God," or sit down and read one of my Alateen books. Help is available. All I have to do is ask.

Things to Think About

"I chose to tolerate a great deal of unacceptable behavior because I was unwilling to admit that I needed help."

Courage to Change, p. 178

To me the Fifth Step meant surrender. Having grown up with the idea that I was the perfect daughter, perfect friend, and perfect student, the wording of Step Five sounded like I was a fake. It meant admitting to someone all the things that were wrong with me.

I later learned from my sponsor that Step Five is a way of acknowledging I've been wrong, and it is the road to making amends to those I've hurt. Although it was a hard road to take, I admitted to myself, to my Higher Power, and to another person that through my over-achieving and perfection-ism, I had not only hurt other people, I'd also hurt myself. I was never content with myself, no matter what I accomplished. Now, thanks to the program and my sponsor, I'm finding serenity by loving myself just as I am, faults and all.

Things to Think About

"Without excusing our behavior, we try to recognize what basic need or fear was operating when we behaved as we did."

Paths to Recovery, p. 56

The hardest Step for me is Step Six, "Were entirely ready to have God remove all these defects of character." It means accepting myself as I am and being willing to let go of whatever stands in the way of my growth.

Step 6

To be able to change, I trust that my Higher Power will remove my defects. In the meantime, I practice being willing. Doing things that are good for me doesn't seem to come easy. It takes pain for me to change and grow in the program. I try to remember that my Higher Power will do for me what I cannot do for myself.

Willingness is the key. Saying yes to my program when I want to say no provides the opportunities that bring me growth. I pray for willingness.

Things to Think About

"Step Six is my chance to cooperate with God. My goal is to make myself ready to let go of my faults and let God take care of the rest."

Alateen—a Day at a Time, p. 23

As long as I can remember, I worried about my dad and what he did. Sometimes I got so caught up in thinking about him and his problems that it affected my schoolwork. I couldn't concentrate and was listening to my own thoughts instead of paying attention.

When I came to Alateen, I learned about using slogans. One slogan was "Let Go and Let God." The more I thought about it, the more I understood. If I would just let go and get out of the way, God would have the opportunity to take care of my dad in ways that I could not even imagine.

I cannot help anyone unless I help myself first. I cannot give away what I do not have. If I concentrate on what is my responsibility, like my homework, I will do much better and I'll give God room to work.

Things to Think About

"If I'm trying to carry people instead of the message of the program, I could be hurting a lot of people, including me."

Alateen—a Day at a Time, p. 213

When I get angry or lose my temper, my mind goes blank and I end up arguing or physically fighting. When I can remember to use the slogans "Easy Does It" and 'How Important Is It?" I can gain control over my anger. I've never been able to do that before! Controlling my anger can help me stay out of trouble, especially with the alcoholic.

If I can remember to apply my slogans and use my program, I can stay out of hot water with the alcoholic and everybody else.

Things to Think About

"Saying 'How Important Is It?' can help us to be cool under stress. That way we can save energy for the things that really matter."

Alateen—Hope for Children of Alcoholics, p. 52

"This Too Shall Pass" is a saying that I use frequently. I use it for all the bad things that happen in my life. When I'm having a bad day or week or month, I tell myself, "This Too Shall Pass" and try to

remember that tomorrow is another day. This works well for me because it encourages me to look past the discomfort of the situation and toward hope.

One day I realized that it isn't just to the bad things that these words apply, but to good things, too. When I'm having a really good day, I remind myself that "This Too Shall Pass" so I can cherish the good moments, such as a pause in my parent's drinking, and not take the good things for granted. A good moment passes as quickly as a bad one does.

Things to Think About

When I view my days as a series of opportunities and possibilities, rather than problems and difficulties, it is easier for me to accept the good things life has to offer and to let the bad things pass.

I came to the meetings thinking that the program would fix me, but that is not how it works.

The program only gives me the tools. It is up to me to do the work. The same is true for the alcoholic in my life. He needs to want to change and to use the tools to get better. It doesn't just happen all at once. It takes a while, and that's why I have to take life one day at a time.

In Alateen I learn to help myself and let the alcoholic do the same. The group members can help me get through hard times.

Things to Think About

"I just can't pray and expect to get answers immediately. But I can look for them among the members of my Alateen group, in the literature I read, and in a lot of other places.

The key is to start looking."

Alateen—a Day at a Time, p. 269

T
R
A
D
I
T
I
O
N

1
0

Al-Anon and Alateen do not get involved in outside issues. Outside issues include politics and religion. We are a spiritual organization, but we are not affiliated with any religion or political point of view. If Alateen were strictly of one faith, for example, that requirement would eliminate a lot of potential members. It would be a loss to Alateen and it would scare off people who really wanted our help. All young people who are affected by someone else's drinking are welcome to belong to Alateen. Tradition Ten helps to guarantee that.

Things to Think About

"The Alateen Groups have no opinion on outside issues; hence our name ought never be drawn into public controversy."

Alateen Tradition Ten

I was full of doubt when I decided it was time to transition from Alateen to Al-Anon. My home group was relatively small, normally consisting of between five and ten members. I had been the group representative and was the longest-attending member. I was afraid to leave my Alateen group because it was so small and had so many newcomers. I was sure it would fall apart without me! I also doubted that I would ever fit in at Al-Anon meetings.

My fears were put to rest when another member from my Alateen group took over my position as group representative. At the same time, my Al-Anon group welcomed me with open arms. Any fears I had were lessened as I experienced the real reason for me to be in the Al-Anon program—to share my experience, strength, and hope.

Things to Think About

". . . many Alateen members suggest attending both Alateen and Al-Anon meetings until fully ready to 'let go.' Alateen members say, 'You'll know when the time is right.'"

Moving On! From Alateen to Al-Anon, p. 3

Before I came to Alateen, I used to worry a lot about what other people thought of me. I hid behind a mask and never really shared my true feelings.

At my first meeting, all this stuff just started pouring out. I felt as though a huge weight had lifted off my shoulders. It was great! I couldn't believe the feedback I was getting. People actually identified with what I was saying.

Now I realize that my true friends are the ones who accept me for myself. I'm a worthwhile person and I don't have to believe it when other people tell me differently.

Trusting other people is hard, but if I keep talking things over with my Alateen friends, I'll find that I'm not alone with these problems. Today I can trust other people and give myself a chance to feel some of the serenity that this program has to offer.

Things to Think About

"I've learned to love and respect myself. Most of all, I know that I'm important and that people will be there when I need them."

Alateen Talks Back on Higher Power, p. 27

The last few years when my mom was married to my stepfather, he became very abusive to me, my mom, and my younger brothers. I never understood why my mom chose to keep us in that alcoholic environment. I lost a lot of respect for her. When she finally decided to divorce my stepdad, she moved my brothers and me halfway across the country. Again I resented her big time.

It has taken a long time in Alateen for me to understand that my mom was doing the best she could to make the right decision for me and my brothers. She also grew up in a troubled family. It took a lot for her to start over and raise three kids. Now that I realize how much she has gone through, I have a new respect for her. I am trying to learn from my mom and from my program so that I will not pass my behavior on to my own kids someday.

Things to Think About

I have to give things and people a chance before I judge them. I try to understand them and know what they are like, to love them for who they are—not for who I want them to be.

Alateens share on acceptance:

• I heard at an Alateen meeting that I needed acceptance to cope with my problems, so I went home that night and thought about acceptance. The next week, I went back to Alateen thinking that I had it—that I had accepted my family. But I found out it takes more time to learn acceptance, and it just doesn't happen overnight. Weeks have gone by now and I think I'm getting better, but my progress is slow.

• I came to Alateen because my mom made me. I was so afraid of not being accepted, but the members accepted me for who I am, not for how I looked. There was no judgment or criticism, and for once in my life I realized that I am a person too. I could share my feelings and Alateens listened. I found love—unconditional love—and that is why I keep coming back.

• Before I came to Alateen, I didn't think I had a reason for living. My dad died from the disease of alcoholism, and afterward my life didn't mean much to me. My mom made me come to Alateen. I didn't want to come at first, but I decided to keep an open mind. I liked what I heard, so I came back. I've been in the program for six months, and my life is important to me today.

Things to Think About

"I have learned to accept things for what they are. This is so important."

Alateen—Hope for Children of Alcoholics, p. 73

I started coming to Alateen because my parents were alcoholics. After watching their behavior and watching other teens drink, I said I would never drink! But the more I saw and felt their influence, the more I knew that I would drink, too.

Then I started going to Alateen. I felt myself becoming happy. I began to understand that I was affected by a family illness and that I could only be helped if I wanted to be. While I can understand the way people start using alcohol to help them survive, I choose not to follow their example. Alateen gives me the survival skills I need. I have people who are interested in my problems and really care about me. They are there for me when I'm going through a rough time and help me get from problems to solutions.

I don't need to drink to have a good time or to cope with life. I'm grateful that today I know I have choices.

Things to Think About

"Alcoholism is a cunning, powerful, baffling disease not only for the alcoholic but for all the people who associate with the alcoholic."

From Survival to Recovery, p. 16

I was angry, cynical, and a jerk to be around. Whenever my mom would tell me to do something, I would try to get out of it. It didn't matter what it was, even walking the dog or getting up in the morning. I would argue or just do it halfway. I found some way to rebel against doing anything that someone else wanted me to do.

I tried my hardest to keep from coming to Alateen. After a while, I decided to give it a try. I didn't expect to find such caring in the meetings, mostly because I didn't think that much caring existed. I was amazed to find other people who had the same problems that I did. I lost the feeling that I was the only one. I am no longer alone, and that really matters.

Before Alateen I thought nobody cared about me, so it didn't matter whether I did. Alateen taught me that people do care about me and what I do with my life. I also learned that rebellion is not progress. Taking responsibility for what I do and doing what is healthy for me is making me a happier person. It feels good.

Things to Think About

"I stopped looking for things in other people to pick at. I was looking for things in myself."

Alateen—Hope for Children of Alcoholics, p. 87

Alateens share on anonymity:

• Anonymity is Alateen's way of saying, "Hey, say what's in your heart and mind. You don't have to be afraid of gossip here." Gossip would break down the whole anonymity process. Without anonymity I don't believe I would be where I am today.

• Before Alateen I was a troubled person. I didn't believe I could say what I needed to say without fear of criticism, gossip, or people laughing at me. Anonymity allows me to talk about anything. Alateens are here to listen to what I have to say. They take what they like and leave the rest.

Things to Think About

"Anonymity not only protects those we love from possible harm due to prejudice and ignorance, but it helps us to remember that Alateen is made up of equals."

Twelve Steps and Twelve Traditions for Alateen, p. 46

When I had about a year in Alateen, a newcomer came to my group and did some obnoxious things.

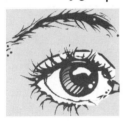 I thought he was rude, and I held some resentments over that.

Later when I looked at my own behavior, I realized mine wasn't very good either, so I changed my attitude. I expected him to change, too. When he didn't, I got mad all over again. Finally I decided to let go and let God. It helped me to concentrate on my own behavior and let go of his. When I can let go and let God, I have time to think about more important things and to take better care of myself.

Things to Think About

"When I hide my resentment, I'm the one who gets hurt. I need to get rid of it before it does even more damage. The Fourth Step is a good place to start. It will help me to see what's causing my resentment and get me started on working it out."

Alateen—a Day at a Time, p. 177

Sometimes I get into thinking that someone else is to blame for everything that has gone wrong in my life. I start hating people for what they've done to me and holding grudges instead of accepting that everyone makes mistakes, including me.

Someone once said to me, "There are no victims, only volunteers." When I stop and think about an uncomfortable situation, I realize that most of the time I have played a part, no matter how small. Realizing this makes it easier to understand and forgive the other person.

In Alateen I learned that I cannot change or control anyone but me. When I take the time to think about the part I've played in my relationships, I learn about myself and grow from it.

Things to Think About

"Sometimes, blame is just an excuse to keep busy so that I don't have to feel the discomfort of my powerlessness."

Courage to Change, p. 189

Our Alateen group has grown suddenly since school started. Some of our regular members feel that things are changing too much and they don't like it. I always wanted the group to grow, but sometimes I also long for the "good old days" when we had eight to ten members who knew each other well. We felt bonded and close. Some of our old members resent some of the new members and say the new members aren't coming for the right reasons. Several of the old members have stopped attending because of this situation. I understand their reaction.

We need to use the Twelfth Tradition to solve the problem. It talks about principles over personalities. We need to remember that we are much more alike than we are different. We have a common problem and are here to find solutions, not to judge each other. If we don't grow and change with our group, we will be left behind.

TRADITION 12

Things to Think About

"Placing the welfare of the group first and applying the principles of the program to ourselves, in spite of difficulties with troublesome personalities, will insure our growth."

Twelve Steps and Twelve Traditions for Alateen, p. 47

Before I came to Alateen, I had a very difficult time understanding my parents. We would joke around a lot, but sometimes the jokes became serious. I didn't know what to expect. My father doesn't drink now, but he's still unpredictable.

The Tools of the Program

Now I don't fight with my dad as much as I used to. We still get our communications crossed every now and then. I love him very much, even though sometimes I don't like him. When we fight, I say to myself, "How Important Is It?" It's like taking a mini Fourth Step because I examine the situation and see what I did. What is my part of the problem? Is it really important enough to fight about?

Today I'll say the Serenity Prayer to help things stay peaceful. I'll also tell my father how much I love him.

Things to Think About

"If it seems more important later than when it happened, I realize that I'm making too much of things again and I can put a stop to that."

Alateen—a Day at a Time, p. 309

Alateens share on using the program to cope with active drinking:

• The active alcoholic in my family is my dad. When he drinks, he sleeps. Although he isn't abusive or hurtful toward me, he's just not there for me either. I have learned to be grateful that my dad does not abuse me. The people in my group have helped me look for the good in myself and my dad.

• It came as a big surprise to me when my mom started drinking again. It had been such a long time since she quit. How was I going to deal with it? I didn't know where to turn until I found Alateen. There I can share my experiences and listen to others who have been through the same thing. I use Alateen as a positive way to deal with my stress.

Things to Think About

"Alcoholism is a disease not a disgrace. Thanks to all I'm learning in Alateen, I believe that now. I'm not embarrassed by my parents anymore because I know they're sick."

Alateen—a Day at a Time, p. 207

This year my best friend died from experimenting with alcohol. She was not a wild girl. She was trying alcohol for the first time when she mistook the door that led to a flight of stairs for the bathroom door. She fell down the steps, hit her head, and her brain started swelling. She was in a coma for a week before she died.

At first I blamed myself for my friend's death. Somehow I should have stopped it from happening! Talking about my feelings at meetings and with people I trust helped me to realize that I'm not responsible for her decisions, so I started to forgive myself. Now I realize that life just happens and I don't blame myself anymore.

Things to Think About

"We can rest assured that the answers, choices, actions, and thoughts we need will come to us when the time is right because we have placed them in the hands of our Higher Power."

How Al-Anon Works, p. 76

When I first came to Alateen, I thought of myself as very independent. I didn't need anyone. I could deal with my problems by myself—thank you, very much. As I started under-standing the reality of my life, I realized I was in denial about a lot of issues. I hadn't been dealing with my problems.  Avoiding them was my idea of dealing with them.

With the help of friends in my group, I've begun to really solve some of my difficulties. It helped to talk with people and get feedback about what part of the problem was mine to change. Today I can handle some things by myself, but I never would have reached this point without my group.

All of us need other people. I need the group, and my group needs me. No one is strong enough to deal with everything. The sooner I have let someone into my life, the easier things have become.

Things to Think About

"In Step Two we try to find belief in something greater than ourselves. We believe this Power can help us find a way to a calmer life."

Twelve Steps and Twelve Traditions, p. 9

Alateens share on gifts they have received from the program:

• One of the most important things I have learned in Alateen is to stop worrying. It doesn't mean stuffing things or doing nothing. It means going on with my life and taking care of myself.

• When I was new in Alateen, fear held me back. I had a hard time even saying my name in meetings. Now I'm the old-timer at my meeting. I went from not being able to say my name to being able to share in other meetings. I know that when I share I'm helping others, and it gets me out of myself. Sharing is a way to connect.

• I've received the gift of detachment. Once I was in my room and I could hear my mom and dad fighting about me. I tried to tell them I was fine, but they kept fighting. I detached and went into another room and read a book. Detachment helps me stay out of someone else's problems.

Things to Think About

"I have some special abilities. They're like gifts from my Higher Power. But I have to do my part and use them. Helping people will put them to good use and show my Higher Power how grateful I am."

Alateen—a Day at a Time, p. 200

When my parents got divorced, it was hard for me to adjust to a whole new life. It was hard to admit to myself that they were never going to get back together. With the help of my *Alateen—a Day at a Time* (ADAT) book and the group, it became easier.

I'm still hoping my parents will get back together, but I don't think it's going to happen. I have the right to hope anyway. I deal with divorce by reading my Alateen literature, going to meetings, and talking to my group about what's going on. I know I'll get through this, even though sometimes it gets tough.

Things to Think About

". . . while the program wouldn't change the fact of my parents' divorce, it could help me to do something about myself if I'd let it. That made me want to stay around and let the program work for me."

Alateen—a Day at a Time, p. 216

During the past few weeks, I've been very confused. My family has been affected by alcoholism, so I've had problems at home and I've been doing worse in school. Today I took a deep breath and explained the problems to my counselor at school, which helped to clear up my school situation. We discussed where I'm headed and what I need to do to get there. I found that it really *does* help to tell someone about what's going on in my life, especially a person I can trust, someone who won't turn what I say into gossip.

Without Alateen I would never have been honest with the counselor. Talking to other Alateens has taught me to trust and to let other people try to help me.

I think, "Easy Does It!" I think about what's really good for me and then think about what's good for others. If I've had a bad day, I talk to someone. Then I relax, take my mind off of it, and things get better.

Things to Think About

"The great thing about the fellowship is that we can identify with each other. We understand what it's like to live with an alcoholic and somehow the pain isn't as hard to deal with when somebody else knows how we feel."

Alateen—a Day at a Time, p. 98

When I was new to Alateen, I was timid. I really didn't understand why I was there. At one meeting, I was asked why I came. I said I didn't know! Then the sponsor took me aside and suggested that I think about why I was coming until the next meeting. That was the longest two days of my life. She wasn't being mean, but she wanted me to figure it out for myself.

Alateen
What it means to me!

A lcoholism
L earning
A wareness
T eaches
E ducational
E xpectations
N ever underestimate

My dad is sober in AA, and my mom is in Al-Anon. I have three older brothers, and two of them have drinking problems. The disease of alcoholism affects my whole family, including me. I need to come to Alateen to solve my problems and to make my life better. I am powerless over the rest of my family.

Things to Think About

"The best way to help the compulsive drinker and ourselves, is to build our own strength, correct our own attitudes, be kind to him, and learn how to detach from the problem."

Alateen—Hope for Children of Alcoholics, p. 9

The first time I walked into a meeting, I was scared. I didn't know anyone, and the kids were a lot older than me. After a few weeks, I realized that even though they were older, they had gone through the same hurt, pain, and anger that I was going through. I went to my group because it was a place where I could open up, let it out, and still be loved!

Before I came to Alateen, I rode the alcoholism roller coaster of feelings. One day everything would be great, and I would be really high. The next day everything would be terrible, and I would be really low. In Alateen I learned that I was okay, because other members had been on the same ride.

Now I know there are good days and bad, but I need to face them just the same. That means good days or bad, I use the Steps, slogans, and my little Alateen daily reader book.

Things to Think About

"Feelings are a part of us; we can't control them. But we can control what we do with them."

Alateen—a Day at a Time, p. 232

Before the program, I felt invisible. Growing up in an alcoholic family erased my sense of self. I did what I was told or expected to do in order to keep the alcoholic from throwing a tantrum. I was preoccupied with tiptoeing around the house, studying to make the best grades, and hoping I would

"I felt invisible"

grow up to be prettier. But none of these habits made my life happier. When I came to Alateen, I began to understand that my life wouldn't get better and I wouldn't be happy as long as I was living for my parents. That's when I made a decision to start living for myself.

I will try to stop being a robot and living for everyone else. I will ask myself what I want and what I need. When I do something good or worthwhile, I will give myself credit. Only in this way can I stop feeling invisible and discover who I really am.

Things to Think About

What am I doing to take good care
of myself today?

My first experience with Alateen happened when a friend of mine died in a car accident involving drinking and driving. I didn't know how to handle my rage and my grief. Another friend took me to an Alateen meeting.

I thought, "Should I be here? I don't know any of these people. How can they possibly help me?" At first I was scared to say anything because I thought they might laugh at me. But after listening a while, I found my voice and was able to spill out the pain I had been storing. Nobody laughed. Instead they comforted me and shared how they had used the slogans, the Steps, and each other to help them deal with their own pain.

The Alateens in my group have become some of my greatest friends. I can always turn to them for help. They help me deal with my grief and with the other problems created by the alcoholics in my life. Now I know I'm not alone.

Things to Think About

"No one tells me what to believe in Alateen. That's a good feeling, especially if I'm having trouble believing in anything."

Alateen—a Day at a Time, p. 239

In Alateen I have learned that there are two types of giving. One has strings attached so when something is given, something is expected in return. When I give with strings attached, I get resentful if a friend or family member doesn't give something back to me.

The other type of giving is unconditional. This is the kind of giving that I try to practice today. Every gift I give to another and every favor that I do for someone comes from the heart, so it is a gift of love. I expect nothing in return, although I do receive something when I give unconditionally. I feel myself growing, and I believe this is the presence of my Higher Power.

Each time I attend an Alateen meeting is an opportunity for me to give lovingly to others. I may have given of my time and energy, but I have received so much more. I've received honest sharing, lessons in patience, love, and lots of hugs.

Things to Think About

How do I know when I am giving and receiving unconditional love?

Pain, shame, embarrassment, anger, worry, and distrust are all reasons why I go to Alateen. Hope, spirituality, happiness, healing, and recovery are

some of the gifts I receive from the Alateen program.

Listening to other kids share helps me realize that I am not the only one who suffers from the effects of alcoholism. I'm no longer alone. I can share the good and the bad with people who understand. I have been given so much hope that I want to reach out and offer hope to other kids. There is hope in Alateen, Al-Anon, and AA. I feel good when I'm able to share it.

Things to Think About

"Our great obligation is to those still in need. Leading another person from despair to hope and love brings comfort to both the giver and receiver."

Al-Anon/Alateen Service Manual, p. 10

Alateens share on lessons they have learned in the program:

• The biggest lesson I have learned from Alateen is to be myself. Before Alateen I thought I always had to be like everyone around me. I thought I had to talk, walk, and think like them or they wouldn't be my friends. Alateen taught me that I can be myself and still have friends who love me. I can talk my own talk, walk my own walk, and think my own thoughts today. Thank you, Alateen!

• I have a hard time with acceptance. I have to understand that I'm the only person who can change me! If I work on accepting things, I can be happier with myself. I work on acceptance by calling my sponsor and by reading Alateen literature. If I keep working my program, I know acceptance will get easier.

• Before Alateen I felt as if everything anyone else did was my fault. After some time in the program, I realize that I can't take everything so personally. As Step One says, I'm powerless. I am finally learning to let go and let God.

Things to Think About

What are some of the lessons I am learning today?

I remember one time I was about four years old when my mom came home drunk. My dad had put me to bed, but I couldn't sleep. After my mom came  home, she started yelling at my dad and throwing stuff across the room. He pushed her outside, and she started pounding on the window. She didn't know that the other door was open. I ran out to tell her, but my dad yelled at me to go back to bed. He let her back in after she calmed down, but I never forgot what happened that night.

Alateen has helped me a lot. It has helped me by teaching me that I cannot control anything. I am powerless over whether my mom drinks or whether my parents fight. The only thing I can control is my reaction to what happens in my family. I can choose to work my program and keep the emphasis on myself. I want to let go and let God take care of the rest.

Things to Think About

"I still make plans today, but I'm learning to let go and let God. I do the groundwork and He takes care of the end results. Things have a way of working out a lot better that way!"

Alateen—a Day at a Time, p. 184

Alateen to me is like the sunrise at dawn, because it gives me a new beginning. I've learned a lot of wonderful things in Alateen. One of the lovely things I have learned is living "One Day at a Time." When I began to practice that slogan, it was just incredible how smooth life could be when I didn't worry about tomorrow. It felt great!

I discovered for myself that yesterday is a page turned over. I cannot add a new line or erase a word. Today is a fresh new page, and what will be written on it depends to a great extent on me. I may leave behind a good ink mark or even a few smudged words. Tomorrow is unseen. Why worry about it? It will bring with it whatever it brings. It might even be the last page in my book of life. But today is right here in my hands, so I can make the best of it.

Things to Think About

"Worrying about the future and regretting the past do only one thing—they spoil today."

Alateen—Hope for Children of Alcoholics, p. 55

My relationship with my sister was one of my biggest problems when I first came to Alateen. She was a pain! The only thing I thought I could do about it was to keep away from her. Soon I learned that I was just running from the problem. Once I began using some of the Alateen slogans like "Easy Does It" and "Let Go and Let God," little by little, my life started to become more peaceful and serene.

I like to have things my way all the time. When I'm in a bad mood, it's best to get out of my way. I tend to hurt people a lot with my words and actions. Today I know that when I do, I need to admit it and make amends. When I do my part, today can be happier.

I'm Sorry

Things to Think About

What have I learned about myself that causes problems in my relationships?

Before I came to Alateen, I would always believe what people said, no matter what. My dad would drink, and things around the house would get really bad. Then, like always, he would promise to get help. He never did, but each time he said it, I believed he meant it. Sometimes things would get better for a while, but eventually they would go back to the way they were.

After I came into the program, once again my dad said, "I'll get help." This time I let go of whether he meant it or not. I calmly said, "I don't care what you do. It's up to you." I'm sure it was not just because of me, but this time he realized he needed help and he got it.

In Alateen I realized that I have the right to protect myself in any situation that threatens my health or well-being. When I trust too much, I enable someone to hurt me.

Things to Think About

"Instead of getting tangled up in the alcoholic's struggle for sobriety, I can show him a bit of care and understanding and give some encouragement when it's needed most."

Alateen—a Day at a Time, p. 50

Alateens share on using the slogans:

• I've been in Alateen for 11 months. When I first started, I felt weird and wouldn't talk. By about the third week, I started talking a little. It felt good to have people listen to me and then to sit and listen to them. I started going to conventions and they were great. They gave me even more chances to listen and learn because I'm around other kids who have the same problems that I do.

Alateen helps me reach for the stars!

• Today I'm happy because I'm at my Alateen meeting. It's fun to come here and learn to live one day at a time. It helps me in school because I don't get as mad at other kids anymore. There were some girls who took my new pencils. I asked myself, "How Important Is It?" Then I said, "Easy Does It," so I didn't overreact.

Things to Think About

What slogans do I use to help me deal with life?

The First Step was probably the most important step in my life. I didn't like it at first because it says, "We admitted we were powerless over alcohol . . ." It was hard for me to admit anything because I was still denying reality. I wanted to control my dad's drinking, but I couldn't. Admitting I was powerless seemed like admitting I was a failure.

If it wasn't for the program, I probably would still believe that I could control my dad's drinking. Without accepting my powerlessness, I would have stayed in chaos and tried to control a disease. Today I know that I don't have to like it, but I can accept it. I let go and let God so I don't have to worry about it. I know that I have to focus on myself and not on the alcoholic. He will be responsible for his own choices.

Things to Think About

"If I mention something that is on my mind and then let it go no matter what response I get, I am speaking sincerely. If I repeatedly make similar suggestions or ask prodding questions again and again, I am probably trying to control."

Courage to Change, p. 29

When I first came into the program, I went to Al-Anon with my mom. An Alateen sponsor gave me an Alateen packet, so I started going to Alateen. Alateens taught me the meaning of unconditional love by showing me total acceptance.

I started out using the slogans because I could understand them and apply them to small things in my life. I'm working on the Steps now, but I am stuck on Step Two because I like to be in control. I'm learning that I still get to make the choices that I feel are best for me, but I need to let go of the results. Sometimes it works out my way and sometimes it doesn't. That's okay, because I don't always know what's best for me. I'm working on turning my will and my life over to the care of God, as I understand Him, one day at a time.

Things to Think About

"Daily practice is important in anything I want to do well. Why should it be any different with my program? If I make it part of everything I do, I'll start to even out the highs and lows in my life."

Alateen—a Day at a Time, p. 261

Alateen has brought me closer to my Higher Power. I didn't know what spirituality was before I came here. I believed that I had done too many bad things and there was no point in trying to pray because He wasn't going to forgive me anyway. That is so false. Today I believe if I am willing to turn my will and my life over to the God of my understanding, I'm going to be okay. Step Three is hard because I keep trying to take my will back and do it my way. When I do, God lets me know, and I find myself doing another Step Three. God has a plan for me, and I have to trust His will and live each day to the best of my ability.

When I am trying to do it my way, it never works. Praying for the willingness to work my program puts God back in charge. The Third Step brings me back to reality. I may not always have what I want, but God provides me with what I need.

Things to Think About

"We are asked 'to turn our will and our lives over to the care of God *as we understood Him.*' Few of us are able to immediately turn over everything in our lives; making the decision to do so is merely a commitment to try."

Paths to Recovery, p. 28

Before I came to Alateen, I had a lot of problems. I had no parents so I was placed in residential care. While I was there, I found out that my 14-  year-old brother was an alcoholic. I was used to focusing on him and not myself because I was the parent figure in his life for so long. When my brother began acting crazy, I wasn't able to do anything to help him, no matter how hard I tried. The counselors recommended that I go to Alateen meetings.

Alateen has helped me realize that I can't control my brother's life. I am not responsible for his behavior and I can't fix him. He needs to be willing to face his disease and ask for help. I have to concentrate on myself and learn to pay attention to my own needs. I cannot control anyone but me. The only thing that I can do is work on changing myself, one day at a time.

Things to Think About

What has Alateen helped me realize
about control?

Alateens share on the slogans:

• "Together We Can Make It" is my favorite slogan because it helps me learn to include other people. Usually I think I should run the show and that I do everything better than everyone else. Sometimes I even tell people that they can't do something when they can. I need to use my sponsor when I get like that. "Together We Can Make It" helps me at home and at school.

• I like "Easy Does It" because it helps me to calm down. When I get frustrated I think, "Easy Does It." My sponsor reminds me about that slogan when I start crying, and it helps.

• The slogan "Listen and Learn" is my favorite because it helps me to change. My dad brought me to Alateen when he got sober. At first all I did was scream because I was so scared. I picked a sponsor, and she helped me stop screaming and start listening. Now I'm not scared of the meeting anymore.

Things to Think About

"I've thought of other slogans to express the program . . .. But making them up isn't nearly as important as living by them. That's what I'm trying to do today."

Alateen—a Day at a Time, p. 7

The Twelve Steps provide ways to live a new and different life. They help me to know myself. They are like spiritual ribbons that connect me to other people and to my Higher Power.

I am powerless over alcohol. In order to live a peaceful life, I want to change and to practice these principles in my everyday life. I can change, but I need the help of other Alateens and my Higher Power. My old ways did not work, so I no longer want to control everything. I want to turn my life over to the God of my understanding and to trust that things will work out for the best. The program works—if I work it.

Things to Think About

"I don't need to understand the Power greater than myself, only to trust it."

As We Understood . . ., p. 159

The night I attended my first Alateen meeting, I felt alone and depressed. It seemed like nobody could understand me or have the same problems. I thought I was crazy and I hated myself.

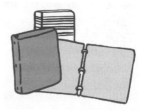

After that first meeting, I kept coming back. I listened to the other members and they would listen to me. I found out that they could accept me for who I was and that they cared about me. I gained self-confidence by involving myself in service work and by learning to write down my feelings. I never liked to write, but I heard if I wrote, it would help. It did, and I'm grateful for learning another tool I can use to improve my life.

Things to Think About

"Willingness is the key which opens the door to a new life for me. If I'm willing to make the program a part of me, good things can happen."

Alateen—a Day at a Time, p. 62

No one knows how our lives will turn out. We're really lucky if we grow up without any big problems. Even without alcoholism, people do not automatically have peace and serenity. They don't even realize if something is missing. When I first started in Alateen, I didn't know that my life was unusual, because I thought everyone's life was like mine.

I'm grateful today that the alcoholism in my family gave me a source of help and hope. If it wasn't for Alateen, I don't know if I ever could have been as happy as I am now. I would have thought that living in constant pain, fear, and uncertainty was normal.

I'm not as happy as I want to be yet, but at least I know if I keep working my program, my life will continue to get better. Serenity and peace are waiting out there for me to reach them.

Things to Think About

"I always have something to look forward to now. There are things yet to come, and I have learned to appreciate the things I do have in my life."

Courage to Be Me, p. 316

Several years after I stopped living with my alcoholic father, I found myself in another difficult relationship. Feelings of anger and resentment returned, but I could tell they were not directly related to my current situation. I knew this time I couldn't continue to live with my self-destructive thoughts. I had to do something to help myself.

Years before, I had seen Alateen posters, but I hadn't been courageous enough to attend a meeting. With the help of the telephone directory, I found an Alateen group. Changes did not occur instantly, but I continued to attend meetings because I knew I needed something. The group provided me with an environment where I could share, feel accepted, and be understood.

Today I have moved on to Al-Anon and I try to apply the program to my daily life. At times it is still very difficult, but I have faith in my Higher Power. I still deal with situations inappropriately sometimes, but with Al-Anon's support, I am doing a lot better than I used to do.

Things to Think About

"The more I keep going, the more I realize how grateful I am that Al-Anon and Alateen are part of the same great 'family.'"

Alateen—a Day at a Time, p. 28

Studying the Traditions answered some questions for me:

1. Why is unity in the fellowship so important? In our groups, we work together to get our lives going. We learn that individually we can't control anything, but by working together, we find help.

2. Why are we an anonymous fellowship? In our meetings, what happens there stays there. We can express our feelings in safety, without worrying about anyone else finding out.

3. How can Alateens attract Al-Anons to become sponsors? We can explain what life was like for us before we came to Alateen and what it's like now. We can ask them to sponsor us.

Things to Think About

"I'll do my best today to learn more about the Traditions. They're the result of lessons learned the hard way. Maybe if we all do our part, we won't have to make the same mistakes and our group will be able to give everyone the help they need."

Alateen—a Day at a Time, p. 107

I am in my transitional period from Alateen to Al-Anon, and I am learning more about myself and the process of recovery. Now in Al-Anon I find myself identifying and reinforcing the program tools that I found and used in Alateen. Al-Anon meetings, literature, and members have become additional sources for helping me cope with anger—showing me how to be slow to anger, and helping me to let go.

There is something else that has helped me. A woman from my mom's group said if someone or something bothers you, pretend that your body is covered with baby oil. This way anything they say or do can just slide off. I let a lot of things I encounter in life and in the so-called real world just slide off.

˘ ☺ Smile ˘ ☺

Things to Think About

"Al-Anon and Alateen are the same family group. The only difference is the age of the members."

Moving On! From Alateen to Al-Anon, p. 12

Before Alateen my family embarrassed me. I didn't want anyone to know my father was an alcoholic. I wouldn't let my friends come over because they would know the truth. I hid my feelings inside, not showing any emotion. I was like a tight little rosebud that was too afraid to open.

I didn't say anything during the first couple of Alateen meetings, but now I've been going for three years and I've learned not to be afraid. I've learned to say what is on my mind and to believe that people will accept me anyway. The shy little bud is opening and becoming a beautiful rose.

It's easy to hide your feelings when you're like a puppet with someone else working the strings. I need to show my real feelings. I've learned in Alateen that people will accept me if I accept myself.

Things to Think About

"Today, when I ask for 'courage to change the things I can,' I'll remember that the only thing I can change is me."

Alateen—a Day at a Time, p. 67

Before I came to Alateen, I couldn't accept my father's drinking. Even for a while after Alateen, I didn't believe it when members said it wasn't my fault and that I couldn't change him. I thought somehow I must change the situation.

Now I know it isn't my problem that my father drinks and I can't get him to stop. I'm learning how to deal with myself and my own problems. I've learned to let go and let God and believe He'll do what is best. I can choose to live one day at a time and to accept my father's choices. I don't try to change my father's actions, but I try to change mine.

Things to Think About

I'm grateful for this program because without it I wouldn't have a clue. I'd still be hanging off the edge of the mountain that I'd made out of some molehill. Now I can live my life without worrying about tomorrow or anyone else and concentrate on my own behavior.

It was my 13th birthday, my first official day as a teenager. I woke up feeling down and blah. I didn't think I had anything to be happy about because alcoholism split my family apart, and I didn't see my daddy anymore.

teen

Instead of staying home and feeling sorry for myself, I spent my birthday with people in the program. They treated me with respect and really cared about me. What more could I want? If someone had told me ahead of time how happy my birthday would be, I would have said no way!

Thanks to Alateen I was able to change my attitude from negative to positive. I took the day as it came without worrying about what was going to happen next week or next year. Thank you, Alateen, for the best present ever—for sharing your love and teaching me the tools of the program.

Things to Think About

"If I'm looking for love and understanding, I don't have to go far. The nearest Alateen group has all that I need and more. It's free for the taking—all I have to do is reach out and accept it."

Alateen—a Day at a Time, p. 41

When I began attending meetings at 12 years old, I was a shy, scared shadow of a child. Out of fear, I sought solitude over socializing. I felt incapable of holding a conversation for any length of time because I had nothing to say. I was deaf to my own internal voice. My mom and I were strangers. I did not understand love.

I'm 19 now, and yes, it's true that enlightenment comes with time, but Alateen was my flashlight. Like many of my peers, I was in darkness, not to the world around me, but to the world inside of me. Alateen pushed away the shadows and allowed me to see my true self. I'm not shy! I love people! I only thought I didn't like people because I didn't understand myself, so I could not understand others. Thank you, God, for showing me Alateen!

Things to Think About

By attending meetings and hearing other teens share their hopes, fears, challenges, dreams, and joys, I've learned that I'm part of a human family. I have the ability to be someone's friend, no matter what differences might be in our backgrounds.

In Step Nine, I am to make direct amends to people I have hurt. I think it will be a very humbling and rewarding experience to apologize for something I did to someone who also hurt me. But

what hit me the hardest is the amends I need to make to myself. I am the one person I would never have thought to include. I wondered, "How had I hurt myself?"

I began to realize how many times a day I looked at myself in disgust and said, "I wish I could" or "I wish I was good enough." Look at all the times I have said, "I'm so stupid. I should have known that!" Anytime I think or say these comments, it makes me feel bad and inadequate. That's an example of how I hurt myself and why I need to make amends to me.

Things to Think About

"Now I know deep down inside that I'm a decent person. I can even love myself. I'm really glad I don't have to be perfect anymore."

Courage to Be Me, p. 127

When I start feeling angry and out of control, I use slogans like "Easy Does It" and "How Important Is It?" to help me deal with my feelings. I also call people on the telephone to talk about it. They help me look at the situation to see what's causing the anger. Usually fear is at the bottom of it.

Because I'm concentrating on controlling my anger and not letting it control me, people have started to like me and even enjoy being around me. Letting my anger out is okay as long as I can do it in a positive way. I don't want to take it out on someone else or myself. I try to listen to my heart more and to stop my automatic reactions. If I keep my anger inside and don't let it out at all, it turns to resentment. Resentment can destroy the jar that carries it.

Things to Think About

"'Easy Does It' doesn't tell me to stand still. It's an action slogan. It keeps me sane, cools me down when I'm about to boil over, and helps me to keep growing at a steady pace."

Alateen—a Day at a Time p. 296

I've learned that blaming others comes from anger. It makes me look like I'm a nasty person inside, when really I'm not. I don't have to blame others or myself just because something goes wrong.

Meetings Prayer Sharing Detachment

I've also learned that everyone has attitudes. Some are good and some are bad. I have a good attitude when I'm working my program, and a bad attitude when I'm either not working it or something doesn't go my way.

I have choices, too. I can either be part of the problem or part of the solution. From now on, if there is a problem, I want to find out what my choices are so I can pick the best one and stick to it. All the readings in our Alateen books really help me figure out what's going on inside of me.

Things to Think About

"Keeping it simple is a perfect antidote for confusion."

Alateen—Hope for Children of Alcoholics, p. 54

I have been going through a lot of change in the past year, and change is hard. I started my first year in college, began working part time, and became very involved in school activities. I have continued to be involved with the Alateen program as well. I need the support of my fellow Alateens, especially as I deal with all of these changes. I'm also looking for support in Al-Anon.

I've learned to take things "One Day at a Time" and to do "First Things First." As long as I follow these two slogans, I can keep some order in my life during my college years. If people make me angry, I try to detach from them so I can keep my serenity. In order to get through each day and stay away from stress, I try to practice the Alateen principles in all my affairs.

Things to Think About

"Life is more than just existing. The program shows me how to live life to the fullest. Today I'll get the most out of living by working the program in everything I do."

Alateen—a Day at a Time, p. 32

Before I started Alateen, I acted out my father's behavior and ended up getting in a lot of trouble. Then I'd make excuses for it by thinking my father was being a hypocrite—he, of all people, shouldn't tell me what to do. After all, he did the same thing, right?

Alateen has taught me that the reason my father told me not to do these things was because he hated the way he was. He didn't want me to be anything like him. He wanted me to have a good life. My understanding of the disease of alcoholism and how it affects our family has given me a new perspective. Today I know that the way I behave is my choice. If I make bad choices, I can't blame them on my dad.

For today I'm going to meetings, talking things over with others, and trying to stop reacting to everything. Thanks to my wonderful Alateen home group and our sponsor, I'm making some major changes in my life.

Things to Think About

"When I took the Fourth Step, I took it on my feelings toward my father. I had a lot of resentments for what he had done to my mother and me and the whole family. It was hard for me to overcome these and I didn't really want to. But I eventually got rid of all my frustrations about him."

Twelve Steps and Twelve Traditions for Alateen, p. 12

Alateens share on the importance of good communication:

Keep an open mind!

• To me communication means listening to others' points of view and trying to explain my own. In my family, this doesn't take place. We usually yell, punish, or misunderstand each other. Sometimes I don't think it will ever end, but when I work my program and think before acting, things usually come out better.

• Before I came to Alateen, I blocked everybody out — even the people who wanted to help me. I've learned that I need to be open to people and not judge them. If I accept them the way they are, they'll be more likely to accept me.

Things to Think About

"One of the most important things I learned in Alateen was to put first things first. The first thing I needed to work on was me."

Alateen—a Day at a Time, p. 328

My parents divorced when I was three. I know by the stories I hear from my family that my father is a drunk. In the program, I hear people talk about how hard it is to live with a drunk. I realize that my life growing up with him could have been very unhappy, and I am grateful that I didn't have to experience it. Still, my father has chosen not to be in my life and that requires acceptance, too.

Program people help me think good thoughts about my father. They teach me acceptance of my situation and detachment from the father I never knew. I learn that the disease of alcoholism has affected me, even without the active drinking. I need to use the program for me. I accept that my father isn't in my life, but I don't have to like it. Alateens help me deal with this by sharing how they learned to accept their alcoholic parents.

Things to Think About

"Other people may not be capable of loving me the way I want to be loved. Can I accept that without resentment and still love them? I can if I'm willing to accept them as they are and remember that real love comes with no strings attached."

Alateen—a Day at a Time, p. 12

I started going to an Alateen meeting because my mom goes to Al-Anon meetings and she wanted me to attend. I thought going to meetings was not really anything I wanted to do.

After going for a while, I realized that I really am affected by my sister's drinking. I learned that many of the things I did, such as constantly seeking approval and acting out against my mom, were my reactions to my sister's drinking. I realize today that I need Alateen for me and that I can work on my problems one day at a time.

When I am at my meetings, I do not have to be bashful or hold in secrets. The other members are there because they have problems, too. I used to be afraid to speak because the group sponsor is my mom's good friend, but I have come to trust her and the group members. I just had to give Alateen a chance.

Things to Think About

". . . I found a lot of kids with problems just like mine. I didn't have to worry about what I said at meetings. Nobody put me down for what I thought or said. I began finding myself."

Alateen—Hope for Children of Alcoholics, p. 64

For years I had separated myself from the alcoholic in my life. I didn't care much for him in the first place, so it wasn't too hard. It was not until my brother got into alcohol that I really learned detachment.

I truly love my brother. All I wanted to do was grab him by the shoulders and ask him "Why won't you stop drinking?" I wanted to drag him to a meeting, but because of Alateen, I knew I couldn't. It was painful to sit and watch him get hurt and more painful still that I could not save him. I learned the hard way that he has to want help, not just need help.

Detaching from a person I do not like is easy enough, but it is much different to detach from a person I truly love. I have to trust that in God's time my brother will find help. One thing I know for sure, his life is not in my hands but in the hands of a Higher Power.

Things to Think About

"I need to keep my own thinking straight if I want to help people. I have to make sure I know the difference between responding to others and taking responsibility for them."

Alateen—a Day at a Time, p. 213

Alateens share on their favorite slogans:

• "Easy Does It." This slogan helps me when I get mad or get in a fight with my mom. I think to myself, "Easy Does It" and try not to say something I'll be sorry for.

• "Keep It Simple." I have been coming to Alateen for a year. At first I could not say my name because I was so scared. The other kids in the meeting encouraged me and never made fun of me. The slogan "Keep It Simple" helped me to say my name. When I share in meetings, I try to remember to say my name because I know others are afraid to say their names, too, and maybe it will help them be less afraid.

• "Listen and Learn." It helps me because I know that if I listen I will learn more, get better grades, and things in my life will get better.

• "First Things First." My mom said to clean up my room, but I wanted to do something else. I used "First Things First" and I picked up my shirts and toys. Then I got to play outside and watch TV.

Things to Think About

"To keep things simple, I'll stick to the slogans. The words and ideas are easy enough to understand, but when they're put into action, they have the power to change my life."

Alateen—a Day at a Time, p. 7

I've had a lot of experience with alcoholic parents. They can be mean sometimes because the alcohol affects them so much. I've had to face the facts and accept them.

Even though my parents are alcoholic, I still want to love them. Sometimes that's really hard to do, but there are people in Alateen I can talk to when I need help. They guide me through the process of accepting my feelings and then deciding what I can or cannot change.

It doesn't solve my problems to take out my anger on another person. When I'm angry or in trouble, I need to talk to someone and get help. I need to use the slogans to help me put things in perspective.

Things to Think About

"It's okay to be angry, but how I handle it is what's important. Storing it up can hurt other people as well as myself. Letting it out in healthy ways gives me a chance to calm down and enjoy life."

Alateen—a Day at a Time, p. 39

Before I came to Alateen, I thought I was the only kid with a family that had an alcohol problem. I used to envy my friends because I thought their  lives were perfect. I kept my problems to myself and never talked about them. When my friends talked about their families, I just listened.

Now that I go to Alateen, I understand that my life may not be perfect, but I am learning to accept it. Nobody's life is perfect. I try to let go and let God and not feel sorry for myself.

When things aren't going my way, I try to accept them. I need to remember to be thankful because there is always someone in a worse situation. Instead of feeling sorry for myself, I can go out and help someone else.

Things to Think About

"I had to learn again and again that the universe doesn't revolve around me. I had to admit that other people could be right, and that my way was not always the best."

Twelve Steps and Twelve Traditions for Alateen, p. 6

Moving from Alateen to Al-Anon is like when I moved from one town to another and changed schools. Sometimes I knew someone but not always, and things were done a little differently.

Begin the journey

to serenity

For me it was a leap of faith to try something new. I had to learn how to fit in, but I knew that my Higher Power went to that meeting, too, so I was not alone. It is a proven fact that I'll never know or succeed at anything unless I try. I'm grateful that I went to my first Al-Anon meeting and began the journey toward the rest of my life.

Things to Think About

"The love I feel flowing from my Higher Power is a love that wants to find expression in the world, that prompts me to feel less afraid, less isolated and to reach out to others."

Having Had a Spiritual Awakening . . ., p. 50

When I was in my fourth year of Alateen, I was asked to speak at a major Alateen conference. At the time I was asked, I was up to it. However, when the time came to speak, I was a nervous wreck! I wanted to back out and forget about the whole thing. One of the sponsors that I didn't even know asked me if I'd like to talk about how I was feeling, so I said sure. He told me the things he does to calm down before a major speaking event and invited me to try one. He suggested that I look at him every time I got nervous and remember there is at least one person who understands.

When I get nervous about sharing, I remember that somebody will hear what he needs to hear. I am only a channel for God's help and there will always be someone to help me through my fear.

Things to Think About

"Today I don't have to be limited by my old fears. Instead, I can do what seems right. I do not have to follow every suggestion or take every offer I receive. I can consider my options and pray for the guidance to choose what is best for me."

Courage to Change, p. 30

When I was 13, I tried to take my life. My father thought it was a joke, which reinforced the feeling that no one cared about me or took me seriously.

Alateen is not the first place I went for help, but it is the first place that has made a difference. It's more than somewhere to go when I need to talk. It helps me in a lot of different ways. I learn slogans and ideas that I can take with me and use at home and at school. It changes the way I look at myself.

My father doesn't think I'm serious about Alateen, but that's not my problem. That's something Alateen has helped me to understand. I'm not responsible for what he does or for what he thinks. I know my father's criticism hurts my feelings, but having feelings is a human condition. If I didn't have them, I wouldn't be real. It's what I do with them that matters. Before Alateen I didn't know I had any choices.

Things to Think About

"Practicing the principles of the program in all my affairs can make a big difference in my life. If I'm willing to try, a lot of the daily ups and downs will be replaced by a steady desire to grow."

Alateen—a Day at a Time, p. 261

I felt guilty because I stole money from my sister. We got into a big fight, and I thought stealing the money was getting even. When I tried to spend it, I didn't feel good because I knew it wasn't mine.

After I was able to admit to my friends in the program what I did, my feeling of guilt was relieved. Now I know that I have to make amends to my sister by admitting what I did and returning the money. It won't be easy to do, but afterward I won't have to feel guilty anymore. Guilt keeps me stuck in the past and stops me from growing.

Things to Think About

"Made a list of all persons we had harmed, and became willing to make amends to them all."

Step Eight

My father, an alcoholic, died about six months ago. I lived with him for a few years, but the only way I ever knew him was as an active drinker.

I still cry sometimes because I always wanted a normal life with him. My Alateen friends and sponsor help me to get through even the worst of times. Even though the alcoholic isn't in my life today, I still need Alateen to help me. I remain affected by the family disease of alcoholism and by my memories of the times when my dad was around.

Alateen helps me to get through many hard times in my life, whether they deal with my mom, my life, or even my father's death. Death is something I can't change, so I live my life for what it is and make the best I can out of each day.

Things to Think About

"If I'm looking for the secret to happiness, I can stop today. It's no secret—I have to make my own happiness. Working the program will help me do just that."

Alateen—a Day at a Time, p. 242

My favorite slogan is "First Things First," because I need to solve my own problems before I try to help my friends and family.

When some of my friends who are not in Alateen come to dump their problems, I listen and then feel like they expect me to help them. I don't have the answers for them, so I can only listen. The feeling that I should be able to help them is my problem. Sometimes my friends just want easy answers, so I need to work on putting first things first—me!

I have issues, too, and I've learned in Alateen that I need to work on them by talking with someone else and looking at my part. When I need to share, I come to Alateen because Alateens care enough to listen and then share their experience, strength, and hope with me.

Things to Think About

I can help my friends by listening and sharing, but I can't fix them.

Alateen has taught me that relationships are the most important things in my life. Everything else is fleeting and can only bring limited happiness.

Alcoholism is a horrible disease, and it damaged the relationship I have with my mother by making her choose between alcohol and me. I learned to be afraid of relationships because I didn't want to get hurt. Today, although I still struggle, I am learning how to maintain healthier relationships.

I live with myself 24 hours a day, so it's easy to get self-absorbed. In order to avoid that, I need to be with other people. I can no longer be content living in the shadows. I choose to be in the sunlight and to join with other people.

Today I know that I can't be happy without a healthy relationship with myself, my Higher Power, and other people.

Things to Think About

"With each day that passes I come closer to becoming a happy, joyous, free child of God. Inside, my attitude is changing, and attitude makes all the difference in the world."

From Survival to Recovery, p. 26

I have been going to Alateen for about a year, and it helps me a lot. One of my closest friends got me to go. He told me it would help me, and it sure did.

At first I felt weird. I went in knowing only one person. The other eight kids and two adults were strangers. After about three weeks, I got to know everyone's name and some things about each one. I started to feel like I belonged, like I was part of the group.

Alateen doesn't try to change me. It just shows me that I have choices. From others' experiences, I see different ways to handle situations with my father. When I'm upset, feeling down, or just need to talk, someone from my Alateen group is always there to listen and help.

I need to take things one step at a time, one day at a time.

Things to Think About

"Other people have the right to express their feelings, but they can't change my feelings unless I want them to. I can't change theirs, either."

Alateen—a Day at a Time, p. 178

Before starting Alateen, I didn't really know the meaning of the words self-confidence or self-love. In a way, I was afraid of those words. I could only see my shortcomings and, at the most, maybe one good quality.

With Alateen I am now learning to love myself, to see my good side, and to discover some of my good qualities. I can appreciate my life and accept myself as I am, both in mind and body. Most of the time, I don't bother with hurtful things that are said to me. When this happens, I try to take what I like and leave the rest. I think the best hope for a successful life is to develop confidence and to love myself. It's so easy to put myself down, but that leads me nowhere. To go and grow I need self-love's glow.

Things to Think About

"I am discovering that I do play an important part in my own well-being. I will celebrate my achievements and be grateful for all I have been given. I am not perfect, but I am excellent!"

Courage to Change, p. 366

Alateens share on Step One:

• Step One is "We admitted we were powerless over alcohol—that our lives had become unmanageable." I finally had to admit I was powerless

 over alcohol, but it took me a long time. First I had to realize that I couldn't manage my life unless I did.

• Before I came to Alateen, I had no idea what the Twelve Steps were. All I knew was that my mother and father were drinking and that I had a lot of things on my mind. My parents found their way to AA and Al-Anon, and I found Alateen. The Twelve Steps have become a part of our lives. I try to use Step One every day with any problem. I am powerless over other people, and knowing it can help me for the rest of my life.

Things to Think About

How do I use Step One in my life?

Before I came to Alateen, I kept my feelings bottled up inside. They'd build and build until I exploded, and then the process would start all over again. When I was introduced to Step Two, it gave me hope to know that I didn't have to tackle my life all by myself. A Power greater than I am was available and willing to help. All I had to do was believe.

Now I have someone to talk to who understands and accepts me for who I am, without judging me. I am learning to trust in people and to believe that God works through them. Each time I trust a little, I am rewarded by seeing it work, and I feel less afraid. When I am angry and I let go and let God, things turn out for the better.

Things to Think About

"Trusting our group and trusting a sponsor are truly stepping stones to accepting a Power greater than ourselves."

Paths to Recovery, p. 19

Step Three is "Made a decision to turn our will and our lives over to the care of God as we understood Him." It was very hard to turn my will and my life over to God. I always tried to do things myself, without help, but things seemed so hopeless, like nothing was ever going to get better.

Step Three

Because of Alateen, I learned that no situation is really hopeless. If there is nothing else I can change, I can change my attitude toward it. I have a Higher Power to go to when I need help in changing my attitude. I don't have to do anything alone.

Things to Think About

"Some people think they have to do everything on their own. I'd rather work together with a reliable source of help, my Higher Power."

Alateen—a Day at a Time, p. 310

Without Alateen I would be a total wreck. I used to feel self-conscious in school. I had low self-esteem, and my dad's drinking didn't help. He was constantly drinking, but he never hit me. It was the verbal abuse that did the most damage because he was always putting me down.

When I came into Alateen, I didn't understand any of this. That was just three years ago. Now I understand alcoholism and myself much better. I get more out of the meetings. I even helped start a new Alateen group.

During these three years, I've changed. I wear and do whatever I want in school and don't worry about what the other kids do. The program really works for me.

Things to Think About

"I'm worth a lot more than I'm willing to give myself credit for. Taking a closer look at myself, with the help of the program, can help me start to believe in myself as much as other people do."

Alateen—a Day at a Time, p. 88

I like my meeting because I get to participate. I help clean, put the chairs away, share, give hugs, and read the "Do's and Don'ts" card. All of this helps me feel like I belong. I get happy inside when I help in my meetings.

I never had friends before because I was so mean. I hit people, scratched them, and bit them. Alateens showed me how to talk to a sponsor about my feelings so I didn't have to act like that. They hugged me even when I was mean, and then I didn't want to be mean anymore. I wanted friends so much that I started hugging too.

My friends in Alateen helped me find a God. Knowing a God of my understanding helps me belong instead of being different. When I feel like I'm on the outside looking in, I can ask myself, "What am I doing to participate?" Then I ask God to help me get involved.

Things to Think About

"Participation is the key to harmony."

Concept Four

At the beginning I went to Alateen meetings because of my mom. Today I go to meetings because that's what I want to do. I've finally admitted that I am powerless over alcohol. I realize how much help I'm receiving through Alateen. The help comes when I openly share with others and then listen, trying to apply what they say to my own problems. I get help by opening up in the meetings without holding back all my hurt.

TRADITION **T**WELVE

I don't have to be afraid of what I say. Alateen provides anonymity, which means that people don't talk about my problems to the rest of world, and I don't talk about theirs. This principle of the program helps me feel secure. It is my responsibility to follow Tradition Twelve and protect the anonymity of other people.

Things to Think About

"Anonymity is the spiritual foundation of all our Traditions, ever reminding us to place principles above personalities."

Tradition Twelve

I know that soon I'm going to make my transition from Alateen to Al-Anon, so I'm trying to make it to some Al-Anon meetings. Each time I've been to one, I've been fortunate enough to find a very good meeting. I even spoke at one of them.

My biggest fear is that Al-Anons won't accept me. Most of the meetings I've attended have a lot of old-timers with years of program under their belts. I've been in the program for five years, but I feel like they have so much more wisdom than I do. I'm afraid they will look down on me because I'm so young.

I know I shouldn't worry about what others think of me and that worrying about people-pleasing is not being fair to myself. Al-Anons are coming to the meetings for their own good and maybe what I can offer is exactly what they need to hear. I'm going to trust that my Higher Power will take over. I'll try to remember that we're all there because we're affected by someone else's drinking.

Things to Think About

"Age is no barrier because the program is our common bond. It draws us together as we help each other recover and grow."

Alateen—a Day at a Time, p. 297

I'm a 15-year-old high school student, and my father is an alcoholic. It's hard to accept my father's behavior. This is the person I want to look up to and try to be like, but I can't.

My solution is Alateen. When I can't get to a meeting in person, I go to an on-line meeting. I can read the stories and relate to the other kids. They encourage me to be strong and to try to face my own life instead of constantly focusing on someone else.

I'm learning to accept that alcoholism is a disease and that my dad is sick, not weak. Being strong doesn't mean I have to do everything myself. It means I have enough courage to reach out for help. Knowing that other teens have learned to deal with it makes things a little easier. Today I have hope.

Things to Think About

"I know that my alcoholic parent is sick and realize that it's the illness I hate, not him. I no longer have to let that illness rule my life. Now that I recognize it, I can detach with love and let my anger and hate disappear."

Alateen—a Day at a Time, p. 194

In my personal experiences, I handle anger the Alateen way. I try to put the program tools to use. When anger creeps up on me, the first thing I say to myself is, "Easy Does It." This calms me down. I realize that rather than solving anything, getting all worked up just aggravates the situation. I also give myself program talk such as "Let Go and Let God." I tell myself this a situation I cannot control and I am powerless over it.

I use Steps One, Two, and Three all the time, because they make me feel better. I also ask myself, "How Important Is It?" Do I really want to let this person or circumstance get in the way of me being happy today? Like a chain reaction, I think about the Alateen Just for Today bookmark that says, "Just for Today I will not lose my temper" and "I will accept others as they are."

Things to Think About

"Just for today I will be happy. This assumes to be true what Abraham Lincoln said, that 'Most folks are as happy as they make up their minds to be.'"

Al-Anon's Just for Today

I attend Alateen meetings in a youth corrections center. My group has about six regular members and I've become very close to them. Their help and support brought me through some rough nights.

I've learned a lot since my first meeting. I've learned that I can't use my father's drinking as an excuse for me being in jail. There were times I would have been glad to sit in jail for life so I wouldn't have to see him again. Now Alateen has given me new hope for rebuilding a relationship with my father.

Although I still have a lot of the same problems, I now have a better idea of how to deal with them. Using the Steps has given me an opportunity to look at my life so I can decide the best way to go. I'm grateful to Alateen.

Things to Think About

"Living with an alcoholic is a great excuse for my behavior. If I let it, it can keep me from facing the real me. But if I'm honest, I'll realize that I have to do something about my life. Today I'll try to stop using alcoholism as a crutch and get on with my own recovery."

Alateen—a Day at a Time, p. 44

My brother and I never really got along, and as the years went by it didn't get any better. Every little thing he did bothered me. We never said a nice word to each other, and this caused friction between me, my mum, and my brother.

Let It Begin With Me.

I tried talking to him, but there was no response. I wanted to change him and control him, but that made things worse. This might not seem like a tough situation to some people, but it was affecting my whole life.

Today I try not to get provoked or wound up. I try to let go of my brother's behavior and take control of my own actions toward him. I try to be nice to him and stay out of his way when necessary. Maybe he'll come around and change his attitude, too, but even if he doesn't, I feel better. Alateen helps me to let go and let God.

Things to Think About

Why is it important to take an inventory of my own actions before I blame others?

My parents have fought for a long time. Since my dad is the alcoholic, I always resented him and took my mom's side. Alateen has taught me not to resent my dad because he has a disease. It has also taught me not to take sides or even get into my parents' arguments. I have to detach from them, put them in my Higher Power's hands, and let them work it out for themselves.

Now that I don't hate and resent my dad, I've been able to have one-on-one talks with him about some pretty spiritual stuff. This has given me a chance to know him for the great guy he is.

Things to Think About

"Before I went to Alateen, I never realized how deeply I resented my father's drinking. As I look back now, I can remember my frequent tantrums, the tension that encompassed the whole house . . ."

Alateen—Hope for Children of Alcoholics, p. 68

My goal for today is to have the best day I can. I can't live the whole day at once, so I have to take things as they come.

This idea slows me down and helps me concentrate. If I take a test, I try to relax and take it just one question at a time. At the end, I'm more peaceful and less frustrated about how many questions I didn't answer.

I will look at the glass as half full, not half empty. At the end of the day, I want to look back at the good things and not concentrate on the bad.

Things to Think About

"Being frustrated paralyzes my thinking. The more I struggle, the worse it gets. The program has an answer: relax and put things into perspective. As peace of mind takes over, there's just no room for frustration."

Alateen—a Day at a Time, p. 112

Growing up with my older brother, I would never have imagined he could be an alcoholic. When he started drinking, it hit me like a ton of bricks. He locked himself in his room and drank himself into a blind stupor. Afterward he stumbled all over the place, scaring the daylights out of me. He was supposed to be babysitting me, but it was the other way around.

His drinking affected my whole family, but luckily I found my way to Alateen. Now I see that I am not responsible for his drinking or his thinking. I want to love him and let go of what he does. Alateen gives me support when my need to control kicks in, and I try to work Step One by admitting my powerlessness over alcohol and over my brother. I need to remember Step One so my brother's alcoholism does not make my life unmanageable.

Things to Think About

"Step One . . . places us in correct relationship with ourselves—when we try to control others, we lose the ability to manage our own lives."

Paths to Recovery, p. 10

When I'm used to something and all of a sudden it changes, it is difficult, even when the change is for the better. I'm learning to live in a recovering household. We're not perfect, and we don't always agree. We still complain about each other, but at least now no one is drinking. We have the program in common, and we're all trying to look at our part in the problem.

I don't have to agree with everything my family does, and I don't have to believe that it will always be the way it is today. Today is just today, and things change. I will change, one day at a time. Thinking too much about the future makes me unhappy today.

Things to Think About

"Yesterday is gone and tomorrow isn't here. Today is the only day I have to live. It's like a 24-hour time capsule. If I take one in the morning, with a 'glass' of positive attitude, I'll relax and get the most out of the day."

Alateen—a Day at a Time, p. 150

When I first came to Alateen, I was really scared because I wanted to fit in. I thought the other kids at the meeting would judge me and put me down because of the way I looked or the way I walked or talked. When the break came during the meeting, a lot of the other kids came over and talked to me. Then I didn't feel like an outsider anymore. I felt like I  was loved, and that's what kept me coming to the rooms and sharing what I needed to share. I learned to trust, and that's the best feeling anyone can have!

Today I need to remember if I don't like feeling like an outsider, the other kids might feel that way, too. Sometimes I have to make the first move. Not everyone is going to be able to come right up and talk to me.

Things to Think About

What can I do to help a newcomer feel welcome?

Before coming to Alateen, I let my fears control my life. I missed out on so many fun things because I was afraid that something would go wrong, so I didn't try. After coming to meetings for a while, I learned that I always lose when I don't try and I always gain when I face my fears.

"God grant me the serenity..."

One of the first things I heard in Alateen was the Serenity Prayer. Now whenever I feel afraid, I repeat the Serenity Prayer until I feel safe again. That way I can take control of my fears instead of letting my fears control me.

The Serenity Prayer helps me remember that my Higher Power will not put anything in front of me that I cannot handle with His help. When I remember this, I can face my fears one at a time and not let them control my thoughts.

Things to Think About

When do I let fear control what I do?

My dad comes home every night and goes to the garage to drink beer. Then he sits and watches TV. He talks and gripes at the TV until he finally gets tired enough to go to bed. My sister and I just stay in our rooms.

The only help I've received is from my Alateen group. When I first came to Alateen, I was so depressed that I hardly smiled. I had already tried to kill myself. In Alateen I found people I could trust who really cared about me.

I've gone through all my Steps, and now I sponsor another member. My favorite slogan is "Together We Can Make It," because I never was able to say "we" or "together" before. It used to be just me. Thanks, Alateen, you've saved my life!

Things to Think About

"Doing Twelfth Step work is good for me. It's a great opportunity to think about all the program has done for me and to put it into practice by carrying the message to others."

Alateen—a Day at a Time, p. 91

Talking to people about past events in my life was always very hard for me to do. Before Alateen I used to hold things inside. I believed the best way to handle the nightmares that happened to me was to refuse to talk about them. Of course, even though I didn't speak of the past, I couldn't forget my experiences.

I'm stuck

Now I realize that I can forgive without having to forget. I can use my past as a resource when I need to connect with someone. I look forward to my new experiences with Alateen and Al-Anon and to the helpful ideas I might share with those who are willing to listen.

Things to Think About

"If I take the time to be a more positive person today, I might be surprised by all the good I'll see around me."

Alateen—a Day at a Time, p. 193

In the First Step, we admit that we are powerless. For me to admit that I was powerless over anything was a big problem. I always had to be in control. In my need to control, I took on all of the alcoholic's problems and felt responsible to find a way to solve them.

When I came to Alateen, I had to learn to let go of control and to realize that the only person I can control is myself. When I find myself repeating conversations in order to get someone to do what I think they should do, I'm trying to control. Now after six years in Alateen, I find it's much easier for me to remember the slogan "Let Go and Let God." By letting go of other people and turning them over to God, I can ease my burden and focus on improving myself. Sometimes that's hard enough.

Things to Think About

"When I let go of my stubborn self-will
and accept the fact that I can't control everything
and everyone in my life,
it's a big step in my own growth."

Alateen—a Day at a Time, p. 20

Both of my parents are alcoholic. They switched me from private school to public school. I had maybe two friends and I was ahead of everyone, so people treated me like I was a freak. I felt like an outcast. Then my best friend took me to an Alateen meeting. I was so scared. I thought Alateens would look down on me like the kids at school did. Luckily there were only about six people at the meeting. I hardly said anything.

After a few meetings, I began to realize that I could say anything I wanted. I could admit to anything or be silent or shy. These people would still accept me. One day I told them how I felt and started to cry. Not one person made fun of me. Instead I was hugged and comforted, which made me cry more.

Some of the original six have moved away, but I'm grateful they were there when I needed them. Now it's my responsibility to be there for the new kids who walk through the door.

Things to Think About

"If you're thinking about going to a meeting, go to the meeting, and think about it afterwards."

From Survival to Recovery, p. 141

The Serenity Prayer has played a big part in my recovery. I use it when I feel pressure and anxiety building inside of me. I also use it when I feel anger and resent-ment toward the alcoholic in my life. It relieves my stress and calms my anger when I remem-ber that along with acceptance comes peace.

When I fight the reality in my life, it makes me crazy. Alateen has taught me to let go of my anger and resentment because it feels like I'm car-rying a lead ball in my stomach, and the only one it hurts is me.

I need to remember to say the Serenity Prayer right away before the anger and resentment can interfere with my daily life.

Things to Think About

"God, grant me the serenity to accept the things I cannot change, courage to change the things I can, and wisdom to know the difference."

Serenity Prayer

I need serenity in my life, and Alateen teaches me how to get it. I cannot maintain my serenity unless I feel okay with myself, so I need to love and accept myself above all.

Serenity is being at peace with myself, my surroundings, and other people. If I start with myself, it becomes much easier to experience serenity with others.

Staying serene is tough when the people around me are chaotic. What should I do? I find the best thing for me is to leave the room, detach, and keep from participating in the chaos.

Let it begin with me. I am the only one I can change, so that's where change can start. One day at a time, I will get better.

Things to Think About

"When I take the time to look after me first, I'm well on my way to finding something I've always wanted: self-respect."

Alateen—a Day at a Time, p. 241

For a long time, I didn't know how to deal with my parents. I just stuffed all of my feelings inside. Sometimes my feelings would explode, and I'd take out all of my emotions on everyone else—which just gave me more problems to deal with.

One day someone introduced me to Alateen. I was very quiet at first, but after a while my Alateen friends helped me to break free. I no longer felt I had to suffer in silence. It was okay to talk about what was going on in my family and how that affected me. Today I'm better at talking about my problems, and I find it's making my life better.

Alateen taught me how to trust and to hope. I trust my friends to keep what I say to themselves. I feel hopeful when I see how other people's lives are getting better.

Things to Think About

"[Alateen is] helping me to get my feelings out in the open. It's the only place I've ever found where I can do that. So that's why I keep coming back..."

Courage to Be Me, p. 311

Coming to Alateen has helped me bring my problems out in the open. In the past, I didn't tell anyone what was going on in my home. I thought it would separate me from everyone by making me seem different. Even though I don't share at every meeting, I feel a lot better when I do share.

Alateen has helped me recognize that my father's drinking is not my fault. For years my dad told me that my two brothers and I were the main reason for his drinking. If it wasn't for Alateen, I'd still believe that. I did not cause his drinking and I cannot control it. I do not have to carry guilt for something that is not my fault.

Alateen has shown me that I'm not the only one dealing with these problems. In my home group, there are 24 other kids whose problems are a lot like mine. By sharing our experience, strength, and hope, we all get better together.

Things to Think About

What does it mean to me when we say, "Together We Can Make It"?

My life was a crazy mess until I came to Alateen. My dad would come home drunk and Mom would scream at him for hours. Eventually she started drinking, too. I couldn't get close to my friends because we were always moving to a different place. When I was nine, Mom divorced my dad and I hated her for it.

My mom started going to AA when I was 12, and I started going to Alateen. Since AA and Alateen, my life has changed completely. It is no longer full of violence and hatred. I'm still learning how to live in serenity, but I have hope for the future and I feel grateful for today.

My future does not have to be a reflection of the past. I can talk about my past to help others, but I am not doomed to live that way again. Today I know I have choices.

Things to Think About

What choices can I make today that will help me feel serene?

I came to my first meeting almost two years ago, because my mother dragged me. We both finally realized that my father was an alcoholic when he had two car accidents and three arrests for drunk driving within a couple of months. We could no longer stay in denial. He went into rehabilitation for his alcoholism, but he didn't accept that he has a disease. He now lives in another town. I think he's doing okay, but he doesn't talk to me very much.

It hurts to know that my dad is still drinking. I have to remember to take life one day at a time and to keep working my program. I can't make him accept his alcoholism or want sobriety, but I have learned to accept him for where he is and to go on with my own life.

Alateen has taught me to take the emphasis off of my father and to put it back on me. Each day I try to apply the slogans and the Steps to my life. No matter what my dad does, I'll be better prepared.

Things to Think About

"It's easier to accept something when I know what I'm dealing with. The program helps me to learn more about alcoholism and myself. That makes it easier to accept, understand, and even love my family and myself."

Alateen—a Day at a Time, p. 319

I've always felt angry with my mom. I thought it was her fault that my dad left and I was so miserable. I didn't know anything about his alcoholism until I came home one day and read his note. He told us that he had gone to the hospital because he could no longer handle his drinking. I finally realized it wasn't my mom's fault that my dad left.

That was over two years ago, and my whole life has changed. The image of my "perfect" family was shattered beyond repair. I learned that there is no such thing as a perfect family. Today I love my family and I'm working on acceptance. I've always been afraid to show my emotions, so I bottled my feelings up inside. Alateen is helping me to work on expressing them one day at a time. I'm grateful that I have Alateen to help me work through my pain and to teach me how to show my feelings.

Things to Think About

". . . I have learned that feelings aren't shortcomings. The true nature of my problem was my stubborn refusal to acknowledge feelings, to accept them, and to let them go. I have very little power over what feelings arise, but what I choose to do about them is my responsibility."

Courage to Change, p. 249

I used to blame other people for things I would do. I found out it only got me into trouble. In Alateen I have learned to admit what I did, to keep the focus on myself, and to stop blaming everyone else.

How Important Is It?

Rather than losing my temper at my brother, my mom, or anybody, Alateen has shown me how to release my feelings in positive ways like writing, talking to my sponsor, taking a walk, or applying a slogan like "How Important Is It?" Releasing my anger in a way that makes others feel bad isn't good for me or for them.

Things to Think About

". . . I'm only trying to cover myself. Alateen tells me to be honest—to be responsible for my actions. It takes less energy to tell the truth and it works out better for everybody concerned."

Alateen—a Day at a Time, p. 265

I think courage is something I'm beginning to understand. About a month ago, I walked into a beginners' meeting by myself, shaking and very afraid. It was one of the scariest things I've ever done. Then the meeting began, and I began to feel comfortable and at peace. I remember telling the group that I had so many fears and worries. I thought the support of others would help.

Alateen helps me hit my problems out of the park.

So far I've gone to four meetings. Each time I get a little more insight and hope about my life. I'm not sure who or what gave me the courage to walk through that door for the first time or every other time, but I'm grateful. What I do know is I can't give up. I need those people, and I hope everyone who reads this will know he or she isn't alone, either. With Al-Anon or Alateen, there is always support available to us.

Things to Think About

How have I shown courage in a scary situation?

Alateen literature on detachment reminds me that I don't have to suffer because of the actions or reactions of other people. Knowing that helps, but it's not always easy to do. How can I tune other people out?

When I find myself in an uncomfortable situation, I have choices. I can detach by choosing to keep my mouth shut, to leave, to say a prayer, or just to be still. When I do this, it feels like I'm rolling up a window between me and the problem. It's been my experience that jumping into the fire of another's emotional outburst will not put out the fire, and it will probably hurt.

The minute-by-minute choice is always mine. Do I listen to the calm, wise voice of my program and my Higher Power, or to the madness of those around me? Life is short, and I want to laugh as much as I can and suffer as little as necessary.

Things to Think About

"Today I'll stop concentrating on the things that are bothering me and keep my mind on the source of my help—the program."

Alateen—a Day at a Time, p. 299

My mother has been sober for three years, and I am so proud of her. She has taken care of me for more than two years without any help. But I still have a family problem because my dad is also an alcoholic, and he won't admit it.

I wanted to shake him and tell him he needs help. I tried that once when we were at his house, but he got mad. I tried not to listen to him, but he said something that really upset me and I had to say something back. Then we got into a fight. I was scared, and he was screaming. He took me home, and I cried for a long time. I've learned that trying to convince him of anything will not work. It will just ruin my day.

Alateen is teaching me that I am powerless over my dad's drinking. I need to accept his alcoholism and be grateful for my mom's sobriety.

Things to Think About

"It never occurred to me that I could simply and politely ask for what I wanted, or that I could accept my request being turned down! But I'm learning. A day at a time I'm learning."

Courage to Change, p. 314

I just graduated from high school and will be going away to college. For the first time in five years, I'm having problems at home. I am scared to death of what is going to happen to my mom. I know I need to go to more meetings, and I need to work the first three Steps again. I am powerless over what she does, whether I'm living here or not. There is a Power that will take care of her, and I need to turn her over to that Power.

I am starting a totally new part of my life. I want to concentrate on what's good for me and do what I can to take care of myself. All of this change is scary, but it's exciting, too. I will look for the positive and do what I need to do today. If I keep thinking about my fear, I'm keeping it alive. It becomes a self-fulfilling prophecy.

Things to Think About

Let me live one day at a time. Why cry for yesterday or fear for tomorrow? Yesterday cannot be changed and tomorrow may not deserve any tears.

Alateens share on feelings:

• Alateen has helped me deal with my mixed feelings. Before I went to Alateen I didn't have a clue. One minute I would be happy and the next minute really sad. I felt alone because I thought no one else felt the same way that I did. In Alateen I found that many people feel exactly the way I do. Talking about my feelings with other people has made me feel better. I'm not alone anymore.

• I feel like a different person since I've been going to Alateen. It makes me feel special. When I feel special, it's easier to say no to doing stuff that I don't really want to do. It helps me solve my problems.

• I feel comfortable in my Alateen meeting. I can share my feelings with others and know that no one will make fun of what I say. When it's time to share, I don't have to hold back my feelings and I can relate to the problems that others are having.

Things to Think About

"I learned Alateen is an individual program. It offers me the chance to act in a healthier way; to change my attitude from hopelessness and self-pity to joy and contentment."

Alateen—Hope for Children of Alcoholics, p. 60

Since I've been in Alateen, I have met many people with totally different religious beliefs than mine. I thought that the way I was brought up was the right way. I thought the way I believed was the only truth.

After many meetings, I came to believe that there is a Higher Power in all of us. Rather than a religious power, it's a spiritual power. I believe in a Power that is greater than any one person. Every day I pray to that Power and I feel it drawing near. I credit my sanity and my happiness to this God of my understanding.

No matter what I believe, I don't need to judge others for what they believe. I can't walk in their shoes because they probably wouldn't fit.

Things to Think About

"Came to believe that a Power greater than ourselves could restore us to sanity."

Step Two

I felt really confused about my dad. I wasn't sure if I should love him or hate him. I know he was mean to my whole family.

Alateen has helped me get through a lot of anger to understand what is wrong with my dad. I'm beginning to believe that he is trying to be the best dad he can be, but he has the disease of alcoholism. I've learned what the symptoms of his disease are, and I can see them in his behavior. I'm trying to love him even though I don't like the decisions he makes or the way he acts.

The program teaches me that I am not responsible for my father's drinking and I don't have to like it. I do have to accept the reality that he is an alcoholic, and I must take care of myself. If I spend my energy being angry and resentful, it hurts me. It doesn't change him at all. I need to learn to separate him from his disease.

Things to Think About

"If I treat the alcoholic with understanding, we're a lot more comfortable with each other and my friends seem to respect him more, too."

Alateen—a Day at a Time, p. 315

The first three Steps are tied together very well. In Step One, I admit that I cannot manage my life, which is a hard thing to do. I always thought managing my life was my responsibility, and Step One sounded like I was a failure.

When I looked at Step Two, though, I felt better about not being able to control my life. I learned that it is controlled by something far big-

One, Two, Three

ger than I am. My life is safe in the hands of a Power much greater than I can understand.

Finally, since I accepted that I couldn't control my life and I found a Power that could, in Step Three I turned my life over to that Higher Power. All that's left is to continue to let Him have control. It's so simple—just one, two, three. Simple, just not easy!

Things to Think About

"Each of us is free. Our Higher Power does not force His will on us. The decision to accept or reject it is up to us."

Twelve Steps and Twelve Traditions for Alateen, p. 9

When I took my Fourth Step, I was scared. I felt my heart pounding as I put the pen on the paper and started to write. All of my emotions began pouring out on the page. When I put down the pen for the final time, after several days of working on it, I felt touched by my Higher Power. It was a very magical moment. I had gotten this stuff off my chest and I felt great.

Taking an inventory is a very powerful tool of recovery. Every night I can take a daily inventory before bedtime while I relax and get ready for sleep. I use this Step to help me stay in touch with my program.

An inventory is a list of positives and negatives. To see myself as I really am, I need to make sure I include the positive. I can use the positive things about me for balance while I work on the rest.

Things to Think About

"So, what is a searching and fearless moral inventory of ourselves? It is a thorough and honest way to describe who we are."

Courage to Be Me, p. 121

Before I moved from Alateen to Al-Anon, I learned how to know and love Alateens. It was comfortable and I felt confident in myself. My fear  was that my comfort level would go away in Al-Anon because I was young and the members would all be older and wiser.

Transition means change, and change is always scary—but it's also a way to grow. I've learned that the Al-Anons love and understand me just like the Alateens did. I find that I love and understand Al-Anons, too, because we share the same feelings. Age doesn't mean anything when it comes to feelings. I'm glad I tried Al-Anon.

Things to Think About

"When I'm stuck for a meeting, I try the nearest Al-Anon group. I find just what I'm looking for–friendship, understanding, and good, solid program."

Alateen—a Day at a Time, p. 28

When I first came to Alateen, I didn't understand about alcoholism. After I'd been to a few meetings, I started to understand what it was and why I needed to be there.

My dad drinks and swears at me. I thought it was okay to use cuss words back at him to get rid of my anger. While he was sleeping, I stole money out of his

Step Eight

pants where he left them on the floor. I thought it didn't matter because no one knew, and he was too drunk to notice. After coming to Alateen, I realized what I did was wrong.

My dad drinks because he has a disease. I can't justify what I do because of what he does. I have to put my dad on my Eighth Step list and become willing to make amends to him. The reasons for my amends will be to remove my guilt and to set me free. It won't be about my dad's behavior, because it'll be about mine.

Things to Think About

"Made a list of all persons we had harmed, and became willing to make amends to them all."

Step Eight

I'm a very angry person. I'm always fighting with my dad, usually about little things like staying up to watch a movie. I usually take it too far and end up getting grounded or something. If I could just take the time to think, I might find it's not really a life or death situation. Sometimes I just need to detach because every situation is not worth fighting over.

Anger is not a bad thing. It's just the way I express my anger that can be bad. When I continue to argue, I always end up paying a big price. I want to remember "How Important Is It?" If I can detach from some of these little problems, I'll stay out of trouble.

Things to Think About

Is what I'm fighting about really worth the cost?

Alateens share on recovery from the family disease of alcoholism:

• Although I came to Alateen nine years after my dad stopped drinking, I can still tell the alcoholism is there. My father attends other self-help meetings, and he calls them his refuge. Without Alateen I wouldn't have a refuge. Alateen taught me how to forgive my dad for what he did while he was drinking.

• Alateen has helped me a great deal. I can express myself and feel comfortable with the other teens because they've all been there. It helps me maintain my sanity while I deal with my reactions to people who are still out of control.

• The first thing I had to learn was acceptance. Before anything, I needed to accept the fact that someone I cared about was addicted to alcohol. I can't change anyone but myself. Something I've learned is that I didn't cause it, I can't control it, and I can't cure it—but I can learn how to cope with it.

Things to Think About

"I never have to pretend, or wear a mask over my feelings. I can speak freely and know that my words won't leave the room."

Courage to Change, p. 11

I live with alcoholics who seem like they're in a deep, dark hole. I'm constantly standing over them. Even though I'm only trying to help, maybe I'm really blocking their sunlight. I need to let go and let God by getting out of the way. Maybe when the alcoholics are ready to look, they will  see the light and be able to climb out.

In the meantime, I need to take responsibility for my own happiness. It's hard to let go and let God, but I know the alcoholic's recovery does not depend on me.

Things to Think About

"We cannot control our parents, grandparents, or friends. We can, however, show them with our attitude what it is like to lead a serene and happy life when we overcome our troubles."

Alateen Talks Back on Detachment, p. 24

I thought everyone had a dad who was constantly drinking and a mom who constantly yelled. I had no real friends. Sometimes I'd feel so lonely I'd cry until I wondered if I would run out of tears. I never thought any problems were my fault, because I blamed all of it on other people.

Then my mom started going to Al-Anon. She said dad's drinking had affected everyone in our family. I went to my first Alateen meeting hoping there would be easy answers. I felt disappointed to find out that answers were like problems. Some of them were easy, and some were tough. The friendliness of the sponsors and other Alateens kept bringing me back.

I've been in Alateen for a year now and I have a brighter outlook on life. I've learned that a lot of my problems were not caused by other people, but by my reaction to them. I don't think the world hates me anymore. Thanks to Alateen, I'm a happier person.

Things to Think About

"When I start the day with a smile, it puts me in a positive frame of mind and the result is I feel good all over. And who knows, it might be just the thing somebody else needs to give their day a lift, too."

Alateen—a Day at a Time, p. 27

The worst feeling I've ever felt was the fear I had about my mom. I wondered if she was going to be

at home and if I might find her lying on the couch dead. I tried for so long to act like I really didn't care. Deep down I knew that I may have been fooling others, but I was no fool.

I recently moved in with my dad because I needed to take care of myself. I couldn't watch my mom hurt herself anymore. There's a part of me that wants to do something for her, but I know there's nothing I can do. I am going to my meetings to help me work on Step One because I want to find acceptance. I am powerless over my mother's drinking, but I have choices about what I do for myself.

Things to Think About

"We admitted we were powerless over alcohol—
that our lives had become unmanageable."

Step One

When I first came to Alateen, I always stayed to myself. I was going to Alateen to make my parents proud because they really wanted me to go.

"Listening was powerful" It seemed easy enough. I went to meetings, listened, and then left. But listening was powerful, and after a while I realized that my parents wanted me to go for me. That's what Alateen is all about—helping me. With that knowledge and by using my sponsor, I've opened up many new ways to improve myself and to set my personality free.

Through working my program, I've begun to see a better me in all that I do. No matter how big a problem I have, I know I can handle it one day at a time, with the help of the love and fellowship in Alateen.

Things to Think About

"I'm part of a fellowship of people helping people. Knowing that makes it a lot easier for me to reach out to others and say, 'I can't do it alone.' Together we can make it!"

Alateen—a Day at a Time, p. 191

I remember many times when my parents were really stressed out or in a bad mood and they would try to find happiness in alcohol. It was especially bad during the holidays. I was always looking for something that would make me feel special, too.

One time I took advantage of my mom's guilt about her drinking. My plan went into effect at the mall where I shamed her into charging what I wanted on her credit cards. The effect of my selfish action was financially devastating. To this day, I regret what I did and I try to work Step Nine by changing my attitude and behavior.

I have to be honest and recognize that the disease of alcoholism affected me, too. I am starting to see how my behavior has been part of my family's problems. I was not just a victim. Today I need to be responsible for my own behavior.

Things to Think About

"If we have trouble figuring out whom we have harmed, another approach is to make a list of all the people with whom we wish we had a better relationship."

Courage to Be Me, p. 148

I knew the city I lived in needed an Alateen group, so I started one. Al-Anon members gave me a lot of help. Right away we had literature, a meeting place, a meeting format, and even some teenagers who were interested in attending. What we really needed were sponsors. I was surprised at how reluctant many Al-Anon members were to sponsor an Alateen group. I heard many valid excuses from members who wanted to sponsor, but could not. Each week I looked to my Higher Power for help and turned it over.

Once I let go and let God, things slowly began to fall into place. An Al-Anon member volunteered to be a sponsor, and eventually so did another. The meeting started, and so far the group has been successful—we've even had newcomers. Whether the group continues or not is not up to me. I know that it is up to my Higher Power to make that decision. Either way, I keep attending and I'm grateful.

Starting an Alateen group takes time; it took a year for ours. It is important to be patient and get as many people to help as you can. If a group is meant to be, our Higher Power will make it possible.

Things to Think About

"When we are in conscious contact with our Higher Power, all things are possible."

Courage to Be Me, p. 166

Alcoholism can ruin my life and the lives of those I love. It distorts the drinkers' thinking and gets in the way of friendships. Even though they may want to quit drinking and really try to do so, the disease may be too strong for them to overcome.

I was a young teenager when my parents returned to drinking, I felt sorry for them, as well as discouraged and very disappointed. I tried to handle my feelings with dangerous behavior and alcohol. By the time I came to Alateen, I was pretty scared and confused. I found a place that felt safe, while I expressed my feelings to people who understood.

Today I find serenity by working the program—using the Steps, slogans, other tools, and by praying to my Higher Power.

When an alcoholic is drinking, I try to have an open mind and keep it simple. Otherwise, my world can turn into chaos again. Whenever I am in chaos, I read Alateen literature and talk with other Alateens.

Things to Think About

"All I know is that things are different now and when I need help I know where to get it."

The Al-Anon Family Groups—Classic Edition, p. 86

It was pretty hard for me to go from Alateen to Al-Anon. In Alateen people were younger than I was, but in Al-Anon everyone is older. In my Alateen meetings, a lot of the members looked to me for help and always asked me to share on the topic. Most of them were so much younger, though, that they couldn't help me if I was having a problem.

In my Al-Anon group, I can help and be helped. If people are having trouble with their kids, I might be able to shed some light on what's going on. I'm younger, and it hasn't been that long ago that I was where their kids are. It's a good feeling when I can help and relate to people in Alateen and Al-Anon.

Things to Think About

"It's good to know that Al-Anon is there when the time comes for me to move on. It's a continuation of Alateen with the same kind of warm and understanding people."

Alateen—a Day at a Time, p. 235

I thought running away would help me escape my problems. Life was a mess at home. At school the kids teased me and called me names. Running

Change the things I can

away was my safety valve whenever I felt troubled or depressed. I never drank or used drugs, but running away was just as hard a habit for me to break.

It took a long time to realize that I have to face my problems, not just run away from them. Alateen has helped me by letting me see how other kids deal with the same kinds of situations. Now I'm learning to look at myself and see what part I've been playing in my problems.

Alateen's Twelve Steps and Twelve Traditions help me understand what's going on around me and inside of me. They are giving me directions and goals that I didn't have before. It isn't easy, but by reaching out and letting the Alateen program help me, I'm finding hope.

Things to Think About

"Sometimes things are still hard to handle and my problems seem too much for me. But now I know that the problems I have to face aren't nearly as big as the Power behind me."

Alateen—a Day at a Time, p. 95

When I first came to Alateen, I was in a mental wheelchair. I felt as though I couldn't do the things I needed to do—like go to school or get a job. I was too busy dealing with the things that brought me down and drained my energy. Then I learned about detachment. But when I detached from all the bad stuff, I felt empty, like there was nothing left.

Later I realized that I could fill that emptiness by starting to get my own life in order. I found if I tried, I could stand on my own two feet. At first I felt overwhelmed, so I applied the slogans "First Things First" and "Easy Does It." Now I'm not only standing, but I'm also moving ahead. I feel like a stronger, healthier person and I have good experiences to share with others.

Growing up has been especially tough because I've always had to deal with alcoholism. Alateen gives me support and love, as well as the tools I can use on my own. Applying the Alateen tools to my life is what's making me healthy and strong.

Things to Think About

"I have changed quite a bit. It's easier for me to say 'hello' to someone I don't know than it used to be. I have real, true, and loving friends."

Alateen—Hope for Children of Alcoholics, p. 84

When my mom and dad used to fight, my sister and I would hide in the closet. I didn't know anything else to do.

My mom started going to meetings, but she took me to the babysitting room. One day I saw kids sitting in a

my sister →   me

Alcoholism is indeed a family disease. When there is chaos in my home, my sister and I often get into fights.

circle in another room and I asked my mom if I could go in there to have my own meeting. She thought about it and then said yes.

Now my sister and I go to Alateen. The meeting helps me feel better. I get to hear what other kids feel and how they deal with their parents' fighting. My whole family goes to meetings now. I'm grateful because my parents don't fight very much anymore, but when they do, I don't have to hide. I can just go into another room and read my books.

Things to Think About

"I go to meetings now because I want to. It's helping me to become a better person."

Alateen—a Day at a Time, p. 189

When I first came to Alateen, I didn't know anybody, so it was scary. I found out about Alateen from my dad, who is an alcoholic. My  dad knew these people whose daughter went there, so I went with her. When I found out about picking a sponsor, that was hard, too, because I didn't know anybody. I didn't trust anyone! I kept coming back because I liked it there and I started feeling better about myself.

Eventually I took the risk and asked someone to be my sponsor. It was a big risk to start trusting someone I didn't know, but I tried it and I'm glad it worked. Sponsorship is having a special friend that I can talk to about everything.

Things to Think About

Have I tried getting a sponsor or being a sponsor?

Life in my alcohol-affected family was hectic, but I couldn't admit it because I thought I should always be in control. I was so busy thinking about tomorrow that I never paid attention to what was happening today.

My mom had big plans for me. She kept talking about my master's degree when I was only a sophomore in high school. I felt trapped in a future that I might not want. I couldn't find a way to tell Mom that her plan for me wasn't what I wanted.

Thanks to my Alateen meetings, I began to understand that I don't have to figure everything out right now. If I take life one day at a time and be honest with myself and others, everything will work out okay. By taking good care of myself today, I'll be ready to face whatever tomorrow brings.

Things to Think About

"What's down the road for me? I'm not sure, but now I know I don't have to be afraid to face it. Today is the day that counts, and thanks to the program, I have a great way to make the most of it."

Alateen—a Day at a Time, p. 90

THE SERENITY PRAYER

Alateens read this prayer at most group meetings, and members often analyze it during group discussions. It also serves as inspiration to individual members during their daily meditation.

God, grant me the serenity to accept the things I cannot change, courage to change the things I can, and wisdom to know the difference.

THE SLOGANS OF AL-ANON

Alateens use these slogans to seek spiritual guidance and serenity, similar to the way they use the Serenity Prayer. Groups use the slogans as subjects for meetings. Individual members use them to help deal with conflicts, challenges, and as reminders during times of stress. Listed below are the slogans in this book.

Easy Does It
First Things First
How Important Is It?
Just for Today
Keep It Simple
Let Go and Let God
Let It Begin with Me
Listen and Learn
Live and Let Live
One Day at a Time
Think
Together We Can Make It

THE TWELVE STEPS OF ALATEEN

1. We admitted we were powerless over alcohol—that our lives had become unmanageable.
2. Came to believe that a Power greater than ourselves could restore us to sanity.
3. Made a decision to turn our will and our lives over to the care of God *as we understood Him.*
4. Made a searching and fearless moral inventory of ourselves.
5. Admitted to God, to ourselves, and to another human being the exact nature of our wrongs.
6. Were entirely ready to have God remove all these defects of character.
7. Humbly asked Him to remove our shortcomings.
8. Made a list of all persons we had harmed, and became willing to make amends to them all.
9. Made direct amends to such people wherever possible, except when to do so would injure them or others.
10. Continued to take personal inventory and when we were wrong promptly admitted it.
11. Sought through prayer and meditation to improve our conscious contact with God *as we understood Him,* praying only for knowledge of His will for us and the power to carry that out.
12. Having had a spiritual awakening as the result of these Steps, we tried to carry this message to others, and to practice these principles in all our affairs.

THE TWELVE TRADITIONS OF ALATEEN

Our group experience suggests that the unity of the Alateen Groups depends upon our adherence to these Traditions:

1. Our common welfare should come first; personal progress for the greatest number depends upon unity.
2. For our group purpose there is but one authority—a loving God as He may express Himself in our group conscience. Our leaders are but trusted servants; they do not govern.
3. The only requirement for membership is that there be a problem of alcoholism in a relative or friend. The teenage relatives of alcoholics, when gathered together for mutual aid, may call themselves an Alateen Group provided that, as a group, they have no other affiliation.
4. Each group should be autonomous, except in matters affecting other Alateen and Al-Anon Family Groups or AA as a whole.
5. Each Alateen Group has but one purpose: to help other teenagers of alcoholics. We do this by practicing the Twelve Steps of AA *ourselves* and by encouraging and understanding the members of our immediate families.
6. Alateens, being part of Al-Anon Family Groups, ought never endorse, finance or lend our name to any outside enterprise, lest problems of money, property and prestige divert us from our primary spiritual aim. Although a separate entity, we should always cooperate with Alcoholics Anonymous.
7. Every group ought to be fully self-supporting, declining outside contributions.
8. Alateen Twelfth-Step work should remain forever nonprofessional, but our service centers may employ special workers.
9. Our groups, as such, ought never be organized; but we may create service boards or committees directly responsible to those they serve.

10. The Alateen Groups have no opinion on outside issues; hence our name ought never be drawn into public controversy.
11. Our public relations policy is based on attraction rather than promotion; we need always maintain personal anonymity at the level of press, radio, TV and films. We need guard with special care the anonymity of all AA members.
12. Anonymity is the spiritual foundation of all our Traditions, ever reminding us to place principles above personalities.

THE TWELVE CONCEPTS OF SERVICE

The Twelve Steps and Traditions are guides for personal growth and group unity. The Twelve Concepts are guides for service. They show how Twelfth-Step work can be done on a broad scale and how members of a World Service Office can relate to each other and to the groups, through a World Service Conference, to spread Al-Anon's message worldwide.

1. The ultimate responsibility and authority for Al-Anon world services belongs to the Al-Anon groups.
2. The Al-Anon Family Groups have delegated complete administrative and operational authority to their Conference and its service arms.
3. The Right of Decision makes effective leadership possible.
4. Participation is the key to harmony.
5. The Rights of Appeal and Petition protect minorities and assure that they be heard.
6. The Conference acknowledges the primary administrative responsibility of the Trustees.
7. The Trustees have legal rights while the rights of the Conference are traditional.
8. The Board of Trustees delegates full authority for routine management of the Al-Anon Headquarters to its Executive Committees.

9. Good personal leadership at all service levels is a necessity. In the field of world service the Board of Trustees assumes the primary leadership.

10. Service responsibility is balanced by carefully defined service authority and double-headed management is avoided.

11. The World Service Office is composed of standing committees, executives and staff members.

12. The spiritual foundation for Al-Anon's world services is contained in the General Warranties of the Conference, Article 12 of the Charter.

GENERAL WARRANTIES

In all its proceedings the World Service Conference of Al-Anon shall observe the spirit of the Traditions:

1. *that only sufficient operating funds, including an ample reserve, be its prudent financial principle;*

2. *that no Conference member shall be placed in unqualified authority over other members;*

3. *that all decisions be reached by discussion, vote, and whenever possible, by unanimity;*

4. *that no Conference action ever be personally punitive or an incitement to public controversy;*

5. *that though the Conference serves Al-Anon, it shall never perform any act of government; and that, like the fellowship of Al-Anon Family Groups which it serves, it shall always remain democratic in thought and action.*